GOLDFISH & KOI
IN YOUR HOME

BY DR. HERBERT R. AXELROD AND WILLIAM VORDERWINKLER

Distributed in the UNITED STATES by T.F.H. Publications, Inc., 211 West Sylvania Avenue, Neptune City, NJ 07753; in CANADA by H & L Pet Supplies Inc., 27 Kingston Crescent, Kitchener, Ontario N2B 2T6; Rolf C. Hagen Ltd., 3225 Sartelon Street, Montreal 382 Quebec; in ENGLAND by T.F.H. Publications Limited, 4 Kier Park, Ascot, Berkshire SL5 7DS; in AUSTRALIA AND THE SOUTH PACIFIC by T.F.H. (Australia) Pty. Ltd., Box 149, Brookvale 2100 N.S.W., Australia; in NEW ZEALAND by Ross Haines & Son, Ltd., 18 Monmouth Street, Grey Lynn, Auckland 2 New Zealand; in SINGAPORE AND MALAYSIA by MPH Distributors (S) Pte., Ltd., 601 Sims Drive, # 03/07/21, Singapore 1438; in the PHILIPPINES by Bio-Research, 5 Lippay Street, San Lorenzo Village, Makati Rizal; in SOUTH AFRICA by Multipet Pty. Ltd., 30 Turners Avenue, Durban 4001. Published by T.F.H. Publications Inc., Ltd. the British Crown Colony of Hong Kong.

Contents

Photography
Unless specifically credited otherwise, photos in this book are by: Dr. Herbert
R. Axelrod 141, 161, 168, 171, 173, 199, 211 (bottom), 216; G.H. Messenger
85, 88, 92, 93; J.F. Michajluk 194, 198, 203 (bottom), 207; Laurence E. Perkins
6, 7, 22, 23, 24, 25, 26, 27, 28, 29, 75 (bottom), 77, 79, 80, 81, 84, 89, 106, 119,
122, 123, 125, 130, 135, 138, 155, 195; Mervin F. Roberts 18; Harald Schultz
112; V. Serbin 15, 20, 21, 33, 44, 48; Glen Y. Takeshita 200, 201, 210, 211
(top), 217, 220; G.J.M. Timmerman 30, 32, 40; Yoshida Fish Farms 170, 174,
175, 176, 180, 185, 187

Cover photo by Edward C. Taylor

Why Have Goldfish in Your Home?

Most people, at one time or another, have kept a goldfish in a small glass bowl (which, incidentally, is the least suitable container). If the venture ended disastrously in a matter of weeks or even days, it was probably due to a complete ignorance of the goldfish's requirements. Discouraged by their first failure, many people never attempt to keep goldfish again, and deprive themselves of a satisfaction and pleasure which is experienced by all who make a success of a home aquarium or garden pool.

In the past ten years the tropical fish hobby has become extremely popular, with 20 million Americans among the enthusiasts. For many people, this too has ended in failure, usually because they didn't take the trouble to read a book and learn the needs of their fish. "Never again," they said, and today thousands of families have empty aquariums.

But many of them, hearing that goldfish are easier to care for than tropical fish, are beginning to refill their tanks, hoping this time for success.

The chances are excellent. Goldfish are, without any doubt, the easiest fish in the world to keep in a home aquarium—*if the essentials, as presented in this book, are observed*.

You can keep goldfish successfully by spending only a few minutes a day on their care. They do not require heated water. Nor do you have to change the aquarium water. Goldfish are not tropical fish. Their water will stay clean if you don't overfeed them —all you have to do is replace the water that evaporates. They are hardy fish, and with proper, simple care, they will not become sick.

The cost of goldfish may vary considerably—from as little as ten cents to perhaps more than $100 apiece according to the variety and its nearness to an accepted standard. However, inexpensive,

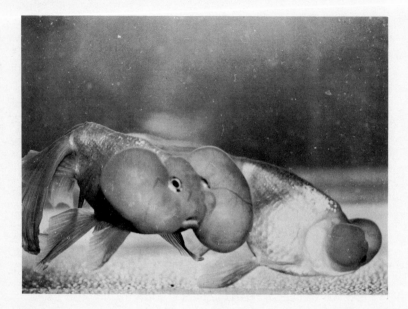

A magnificent pair of water bubble-eye goldfish owned by Thomas J. Horeman. They are said to be worth $1000.

common goldfish provide every bit as much pleasure in an ornamental aquarium as do the fancier types, which may be left for the specialist breeder or the wealthy who consider them showpieces.

In any city in the world you can buy a goldfish tank, gravel, a few goldfish, and some plants for less than $5.00.

These easy-to-care-for, inexpensive fish have become an absorbing, relaxing hobby for millions of people. Is it any wonder? They are extremely decorative, bringing to any home, large or small, a note of color and exotic beauty. The brilliant tones shimmering in the clear water against a background of vivid plants, the graceful motions and sprightly actions, are fascinating to watch.

As with any hobby, the more you know about it, the more

On the left is a fine young specimen of a Bristol Shubunkin; on the right is a veiltail goldfish.

absorbing it becomes. But you needn't start in a big way. Begin with two goldfish, if you like, and as you learn more about their care and breeding—and see how much pleasure they give you— you may want to increase the size of your aquarium.

Don't let the following discussion of the goldfish's needs frighten you. At first reading it will seem like a lot of work, but the actual time required to keep healthy, happy goldfish is only three minutes a day! Observing their habits and allowing their graceful beauty to decorate your home will give you 24-hour satisfaction.

Chapter 3 discusses the characteristics of goldfish, and Chapter 4 discusses the different varieties. First, however, begin with Chapter 1 which tells you what you should know about a goldfish's needs, so that you are completely prepared when you bring one into your home.

1. What Your Goldfish Need

Goldfish have been bred commercially for more than 600 years and have been known and kept by man for more than 1,000 years. This is evidence that these fish, with ordinary care, are very hardy and can live well in captivity—if their few requirements are provided.

TANK

Their first requirement, of course, is a place to live. Suitable tanks, or aquaria, are discussed on page 15.

Tap water is almost always loaded with gases, such as chlorine, that are intended to make the water safe to drink. You can remove chlorine from the water by using commercial de-chlorinizing compounds available at aquarium shops.

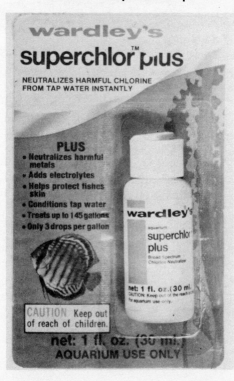

WATER

The next requirement concerns their breathing. Since fish must rely for their oxygen on the water in which they live, you should understand the physical properties of water and dissolved gases in water. Normally, any exchange of gas in water takes place through the exposed surface area. Oxygen that is used up will be more quickly replaced in wide shallow containers than in narrow, deeper ones. While a small fish may quickly exhaust all the available oxygen in a pint of water if contained in a milk bottle, it could be reasonably comfortable in the same pint of water if placed in a soup plate.

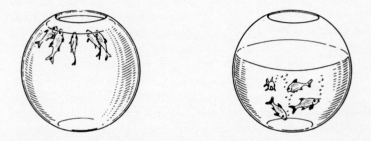

The small bowl on the left is filled to capacity, thereby reducing the surface area of the water. The fish in this bowl are gasping at the surface for oxygen. The bowl on the right, though far from adequate, does have a larger surface area even though it contains less water.

This fact largely decides the shape of the desired aquarium. One inch of goldfish length requires about 24 square inches of exposed surface for comfortable breathing. This, however, is a minimum figure and brings us to the next physical characteristic of water. Cold water will retain far more dissolved oxygen than warm water. On a hot and sunny day a goldfish that is ordinarily comfortable may be in distress from lack of oxygen. A suffocating goldfish will swim with its mouth open at the surface of the water in an attempt to breathe the oxygen in the air. Although most varieties of goldfish recover as the water is cooled, the discomfort will put a severe strain upon them and lower their resistance to disease. It is advisable, therefore, to keep the number of fish in any aquarium well below the minimum recommendation.

For decorative purposes, four fish of approximately 2 inches in length would require about 200 square inches of surface area. An aquarium of 20 inches x 10 inches x 12 inches will roughly conform to this. Not completely filled, it will contain about 10 gallons of water plus about an inch or more of coarse sand to hold· the roots of aquatic plants. Do not think that this is a very small number of goldfish for a tank of such dimensions, but remember that the behavior of crowded goldfish will differ from the behavior of properly kept fish. In fact, you will only discover the true character of some goldfish if the surroundings are to their liking. The fewer the fish, the better you will be able to observe and appreciate them. If you are starting with two fish, a large enough tank will permit you to add more later with no trouble.

(If you are determined to keep as large a number of goldfish as possible, there are various methods of artificial aeration and filtration. These depend for their success on a movement of the water that continually brings a fresh area in contact with the air so that faster exchange of gases and replacement of oxygen is possible.*)

---

*Respiration in water is very different for fish than respiration in air is for lunged animals. This great difference stems from the greater density of water over air and the higher saturation of oxygen in air than in water. Water is nearly eight hundred times heavier than air (at usual aquarium temperatures for both). Water at 68° F. will contain 7.6 milligrams of oxygen per liter, while air at the same temperature and air pressure will contain about 250 milligrams. Goldfish, fortunately, require much less oxygen than terrestrial vertebrates. When goldfish come to the surface to gasp atmospheric oxygen it is usually not because there is no oxygen in the water but because there is too much carbon dioxide and their blood is filled with this poison gas instead of life-giving oxygen.

The aquarist's job is to rid the aquarium of excess carbon dioxide. In order to do this, he must expose as much surface area of the water to the atmosphere as possible so the water can exchange gases with the atmosphere. This exchange of gases, the carbon dioxide going from the water to the air, further assists in that oxygen is then absorbed by the water from the air at the same time.

CHLORINE

Tap water usually contains some chlorine, which can harm your fish if you add tap water to their tank too soon. But chlorine soon leaves the water as it is allowed to stand, especially if the water is agitated by means of aeration or a filter. This is why water should be "aged" before putting it into your tank.

If sodium fluoride has been added to the water in your town, you have a double problem: getting rid of the chlorine and the fluoride, which does not leave the water as a gas as chlorine does.

There are several chlorine and fluoride neutralizers on the market which do a good job. These should be used where there is fluoridation, and may be used to speed up the de-chlorination process where there is only chlorine in the water.

Without a neutralizer, you will need to let the water stand for about three days. Use a wide-mouthed container. If you use a large bottle of the carboy type, fill it only to the point where it begins to narrow toward the neck.

Let us return to the properties of water. Large bodies of water lose or gain heat more slowly than smaller bodies. Since the natural habitat of goldfish is large bodies of water, they are never subjected to the sudden changes of water temperature that occur in small aquaria or pools.

TEMPERATURE

Goldfish are cold-blooded creatures, or, more correctly, variable-temperatured (poikilothermic) so that any rise in the temperature of their water will be followed by a rise in the temperature of their blood. Most goldfish varieties are capable of living in heat of nearly 100° Fahrenheit and in below-freezing-point cold, but they can only survive if the change is very gradual. Any rapid changes caused by the effect of room temperatures on the small volume of water in a 10-gallon aquarium will eventually be fatal to the inmates. Put the aquarium in a room that does not fluctuate between extreme cold at night and excessive heat during the day unless you are prepared to install an electric heater with thermostatic control. When you change the water of the aquarium (if it becomes foul) be sure that the new water is similar in temperature to the old. A variation of five degrees either way will do no harm and is, in fact, beneficial at certain times. If the fish are in breeding condition, a temperature drop of five degrees after a warm spell will often cause the chase before spawning. This is discussed in Chapter 5.

If the water in the tank is more than five degrees warmer or colder than that to which the goldfish are accustomed, it may be necessary to leave the fish in the can or jar they came in and float it in the aquarium until the two temperatures are approximately the same.

FOOD

Goldfish are members of the carp family (Cyprinidae) and are largely vegetable eaters and bottom feeders. You must keep this in mind if you wish to prevent digestive trouble. Generally it is far better to underfeed your goldfish (provided that the aquarium is well planted), for more fish are killed by overfeeding than by any other cause. Live foods are by far the best foods for all varieties of goldfish and a little and often is preferable to large meals at infrequent intervals. You should also understand the nature of the food you use. If the food is alive and aquatic by nature (for example, *Daphnia* or tubifex worms), it may use up the available oxygen if it is not immediately eaten. A large number of these minute crustaceans and worms can quickly cause havoc.

Feeding is largely a matter of common sense. If you provide sufficient food to allow the fish a ten-minute meal with nothing left over, there will be no harm done. A solid teaspoonful of living *Daphnia* once or twice a day will supply four to six average-sized goldfish with plenty of good, wholesome food. For two fish, use one-third to one-half a teaspoonful. You can also purchase quick-frozen *Daphnia* from most dealers; this is a good substitute but must be fed more sparingly or it will be uneaten and foul the water as it decays. Break off a piece and put it, frozen, into the tank. As it melts the fish will gobble it up. (Live *Daphnia* will live in the water until eaten.)

There are other living goldfish foods available to the aquarist: mosquito larvae, glass larvae, cyclops, tubifex worms, may-fly larvae, white worms, ants' eggs or small, cut up garden worms will all be eaten with gusto. (A word of warning: when you use mosquito larvae, be sure to feed only what can be consumed immediately or the larvae may become pupae and then adult insects that will be released into the house.)

If you visit a local pond with a fine-meshed net you may find some of these foods and also have a healthy bit of exercise. However, your local pet shop is a much more reliable source because

A variety of fish foods are available for your goldfish, including all of those produced for tropical fishes. The flake foods shown here were specifically prepared to be used as growth foods, color enhancers, and conditioners.

local ponds may be poisoned with DDT and this chemical, if introduced into your tank with the food, may poison the fish.

Brine shrimp is another convenient live food. You can buy the dry eggs and hatch them by placing them in a salt-water solution mixed according to the directions that come with the eggs. The newly hatched shrimp are excellent for young fish. Both newly hatched and adult shrimp are available frozen. If you use the frozen shrimp, break off a small piece and drop it into the aquarium where it will melt and be enjoyed by the goldfish.

There are many dried foods on the market today, all of them supposedly as good or better than live foods. The claims may not always be entirely true and should be taken with the proverbial "grain of salt" (the claims, not the food!). *Never use dried foods exclusively.* Whatever the claims, they have a high cereal content and you should also feed your fish, if not live foods, such foods as finely chopped fish, shrimp, clams, crab meat, and so forth. Always be sure that nothing is left to decay on the bottom of the aquarium.

Chapter 5 discusses special food for breeding goldfish and Chapter 6 covers food for fish fry.

If you keep two goldfish correctly, you will gradually acquire a considerable knowledge of other forms of water life and gain an understanding of a new aquatic world. It is a never-ending fascination.

2. Setting Up the Aquarium and Choosing the Plants

Aquaria smaller than 24 inches x 12 inches x 12 inches are really more nuisance than they are worth. For decorative as well as practical purposes it is probably best to select as a minimum size a tank about 24 inches x 12 inches x 16 inches. The 16 inches of depth will give reasonable viewing area and also allow some of the taller aquatic plants (such as *Sagittaria sinensis*) proper height for development. A tank 24 x 12 x 16 will hold about 20 gallons of water and will weigh approximately 175 pounds when full. Weight is important—keep it in mind when you select a table or stand for your tank. It is usually best to choose a proper angle-iron stand made for the purpose or to have your tank built into a wall.

Standard aquaria of 10-, 15-, or 20-gallon capacity are quite

This 20-gallon aquarium can be used for goldfish and koi. If the fish are small, this tank could handle as many as 20 fish.

reasonable in price and satisfactory. Avoid so-called bargain tanks. While bargains sometimes last for a while and are adequate in many ways, you can get a tank that will last longer and look better for a slightly higher outlay.

Fancy aquaria are made to fit every decor, and can be "landscaped" attractively. If you want something really handsome and can afford a higher price, a tank can be made to order for your home. Your aquarium shop can help you with custom-made aquaria, and with their decoration, but study your problems first and try to decide what you like and may need for your home.

LOCATION

Where you permanently place the aquarium needs careful thought. In strong sunlight the water and glass will eventually become green with the growth of microscopic forms of plant life (algae), which will obscure the goldfish. On the other hand, if the tank is placed where insufficient light reaches it, the plants will become sickly and die. The ideal position is where no more than one hour of direct sunlight per day falls upon the aquarium. Plants can, of course, be grown quite successfully under artificial light and many aquaria containing tropical fishes use this method as almost the only source of illumination. Experience will show, however, that goldfish require some sunlight if they are to be a success. Prolonged periods under artificial light tend to lower their vitality and reduce their color.

LIGHT

If the location of your tank requires you to use daytime artificial illumination, or if you want a tank light for nighttime, you will need some form of metal reflector. A reflector is usually provided with the aquarium, together with the necessary sockets or fluorescent tube attachments. If fluorescent, no heat is given off.

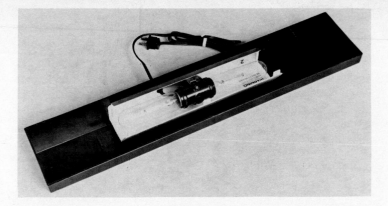

Reflectors may house either incandescent or fluorescent bulbs and come in full-hood and "strip" sizes. The full hoods cover the entire top of the tank and are the more expensive type.

This kind of illumination is best if you need artificial light. If incandescent, the temperature of the water will be raised by the heat of the light bulb as much as 10 degrees. Also, the sudden drop in temperature when the light is switched off at night can be harmful to the fish. (In a modern home with thermostatically controlled heating, this is less of a problem. There will be a nightly drop in temperature, of course, but it will not be as drastic.)

These may appear to be small points, but ignorance of them can easily cause trouble. The power of an incandescent bulb should not be more than 100 watts, or else a blue-green, unsightly algae may develop on the glass and plants. If the aquarium receives adequate natural light during the day, keep the wattage down to 60 or even 40 so that this will not affect the temperature of the water so much. If you need brighter light, you must prevent great fluctuations of the water temperature during cold periods. You can ensure this by installing an aquarium heater and thermostat set at 60° F.

SAND

The next step is to choose the sand or gravel in which the plants will grow. The special ready-washed gravel that is available will require further washing to get rid of all the fine dirt. Because of the risk of contamination, it is poor economy to use sand from

Gravel or sand must be thoroughly washed before it can be used in your aquarium. The easiest way to do this is in a pail. Use warm water and constantly stir the gravel until the water finally runs off without containing any dirt or sediment.

a local river or other source. Though sand may appear clean when water is run through, it may not remain clean when it is placed in an aquarium. The best way to test sand for cleanliness is to place a small amount in a jar of water and shake it. If the water clears immediately after you stop shaking the jar, the sand is ready for use.

The amount of sand required is approximately 20 pounds for every 10 gallons of water. Place the sand so that it slopes upward toward the back and sides of the tank. At its shallowest point it should be 1 inch; at its deepest, 2 to 3 inches. Don't try to have it even, but give the floor of the aquarium a natural uneven appearance. To accentuate this, you can add rocks, but they must not be limestone, sandstone or any other soft type that may dissolve or increase the chemical content of the water. Slate is very good. Whatever type is chosen, make sure that it has no sharp corners or the fish may wound themselves.

Because goldfish like to root in the gravel, they often disturb plants, and many goldfish fanciers have taken advantage of plastic plants as decorations in goldfish aquaria. The,single biggest advantage of plastic plants, of course, is that they need no care or illumination at all.

Sand or gravel should not be too fine or it will become too tightly packed and restrict the root movement of the plants. On the other hand, it should not be too coarse, or crevices will form between the stones where uneaten food can lodge out of reach of the goldfish and eventually foul the bottom. Particles of approximately ⅛-inch will be most suitable. They will form a reasonably smooth bottom and give you room to bring a siphon near enough to remove mulm (feces, dead bits of plants, etc.) and detritus (loose material that comes from the wearing away of rocks) without the sand coming through the siphon.

Undergravel filters are among the most popular aquarium filters because they can be hidden almost completely and require a minimum of maintenance. Undergravel filters must be positioned in the aquarium before the gravel is added..

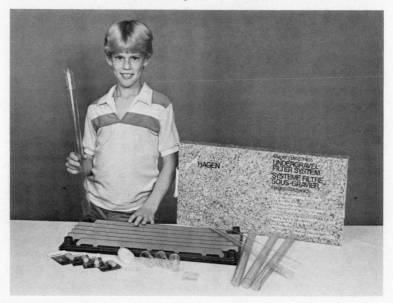

This attractively arranged aquarium is aquascaped with plastic plants and treated driftwood. Live plants can be used but may present a problem since goldfish love to eat certain types of aquatic plants.

AQUARIUM PLANTS

Aquatic plants have three purposes. First, they provide a pleasing natural background and a hideaway for the fish. Second, they serve as food. Third (probably most important), they may serve as a natural purifier of the sand and water. To fulfill these functions, aquarium plants should have a good root system; they should provide the sort of tender shoot the fish love to devour; and their shape or color should add to the beauty and interest of the underwater scene. To get all three requirements you may use rooted plants around the tank sides, purely decorative plants as centerpieces and the more edible plants where they can be removed and replaced if they become unsightly from the ravages of the fish or etiolation (straggly growth).

Before you select your plants, decide upon the types you will use and the position in the tank they will occupy. (If you are using an aquarium heater you can arrange the plants so that they hide it from view.) Do not move plants after they have been planted in the tank or they will not become properly established.

Some aquatic plants grow best near the back and sides of the aquarium where they receive the most natural light. Of these, *Vallisneria spiralis* is probably the favorite. If you buy this plant, be sure it has a good root system. There are three varieties: the straight, the giant and a handsome twisted form known as Corkscrew Val. For exceptionally large aquaria—those with a depth of 24 inches or more—the Giant Vallisneria (*V. gigantea*) is most suitable. Under proper conditions it grows several feet long.

The interesting *Vallisneria* is available in three forms: regular Vallisneria (left), Corkscrew Vallisneria (right) and Giant Vallisneria (not illustrated).

Sagittaria is similar to *Vallisneria* but the leaves are stronger and thicker. The photograph shows Dwarf Sagittaria, *Sagittaria natans.*

The various types of aquarium *Sagittaria* are similar to *Vallisneria* except that some varieties tend to form either aerial or floating leaves. The commonly used form is *Sagittaria natans,* a rather stumpy version of the straight *Vallisneria.* Another variety, Giant Sagittaria, can be used as a centerpiece. Do not choose young specimens because when they are fully developed they will produce aerial flowering shoots that will probably foul the reflector. (See page 17.)

Hair Grass (*Eleocharis acicularis*) is one of the finest background plants but it will take time to become established. Unless you buy a large quantity it is probably best to allow the Hair Grass

Hair Grass, *Eleocharis*, is one of the finest plants for the background of an aquarium. However, it takes a long time to grow and does very poorly if other plants are placed close to it. If you want to use this plant in your tank, buy enough of it to fill 90% of the area in the back of the aquarium. Do not count on it growing too much.

to develop by removing other plants used as a temporary background (such as *Vallisneria*), as they get in its way and will hinder its growth. The Hair Grass will grow into a solid wall of fine green upright hairs across the back of the aquarium. The effect is very satisfying.

Etiolation will occur with such plants as Milfoil, Hornwort, *Elodea* or *Egeria*—all the varieties upon which fish nibble. Hornwort (*Ceratophyllum demersum*) never forms roots, and unless it

24

This is a nice variety of *Elodea.* Goldfish enjoy this plant and chew it down to the stem.

Hornwort, *Ceratophyllum,* is not eaten by goldfish but they spawn among its fine leaves.

is weighted down in an aquarium it will appear untidy in its usual floating position. Since it forms winter buds (tight terminal shoots which sink in autumn and rise again in the spring to produce fresh growth), it may sometimes seem to be growing in ponds from a rooted or anchored position. Careful examination will show that the cause is not the development of roots but some physical obstruction that prevents the bud from rising in the normal way.

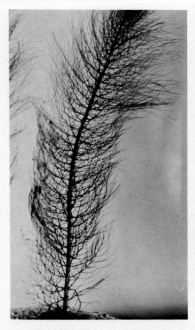

Myriophyllum is a very fine-leaved plant. It is not eaten by goldfish but serves as a spawning medium.

Another variety of *Elodea* or *Anacharis*. It is quite different from the plant shown on page 25.

Among the floating plants, the very small types of the *Lemna* species (Duckweed) will probably be best. These plants provide a good meal for the goldfish and they can be removed if they become too dense. If you don't plan to use Duckweed as one of your plants, it is still a good idea to add a little to the aquarium from time to time, as it acts as a tonic for the fish.

The *trisulca* variety is not as useful as Duckweed; it is not as tasty to the fish and it does not reproduce as rapidly.

Other floating aquarium plants, such as *Azolla caroliniana* (Fairy Moss), Crystalwort (*Riccia fluitans*) and the *Salvinia*

Water Lettuce is a floating plant with fine roots. It is a good spawning medium for goldfish.

species may be more pleasing to the eye but they will not satisfy the fish as well or grow as fast as Duckweed.

There are many other types of floating plants, some of which are very ornamental. However, since they will show through the sides of an aquarium, their root system will not only be visible but may also tend to obscure other desirable underwater plants. Therefore, it may not be wise to add the larger types of floating plants to an aquarium. (This is largely a matter of personal taste. Some people may find methods of arranging the plants in a large, half-full aquarium so that they all appear to advantage.)

One of the most striking of the larger floating plants is the Water Hyacinth (*Eichhornia crassipes*). This interesting plant has the petiole (stalk) of each leaf distended to form an egg-shaped mass, from which the tough shiny leaf rises above the water surface. These swellings, when opened, reveal large air pockets. The interior is like a sponge that acts as a float for the plant. The roots

27

Water Hyacinth is a fine plant for the goldfish pool, but it is not suitable for some tanks because it needs constant sunlight.

grow long and feathery and will probably make contact with the bottom of the aquarium as the plant develops.

Such plants cannot be seen to advantage if you use a reflector, and a reflector will probably damage the leaves. Moreover, the handsome white flowers that grow stand well above the plant and would touch the usual reflector. Lowering the water level will help, but this technique restricts the other types of underwater plants.

The Water Soldier (*Stratiotes aloides*), a similar type, lacks the bulbous floats. When it grows wild this plant sinks to the bottom in winter and rises again to make fresh growth in the spring, but it is unlikely to do this in an indoor aquarium.

Frogbit (*Hydrocharis morsusrana*) is more suitable for the average aquarium as it is smaller and floats close to the surface. It is a very vigorous grower and will soon carpet the surface of the aquarium.

Frogbit, *Hydrocharis*, may be recommended for the aquarium, but it does much better in a pool.

Cryptocoryne (below) is an excellent plant for the goldfish tank. It grows slowly and its tough leaves are able to withstand the abuse most goldfish give any plant.

Another species of *Cryptocoryne*. There are many species available at your pet shop.

The Amazon Sword Plant makes an excellent centerpiece for the large aquarium. The nice feature of this plant is that it grows large enough to fill the center of the aquarium, regardless of its size.

Since the indoor aquarium is unlikely to fall below 50° F., the many handsome tropical aquarium plants may be used, although the growth of some will slow up if they are kept near the low temperature for long periods. The most suitable ornamental center-pieces are the various types of *Cryptocoryne*; the Amazon Sword Plant (it will require the whole center space for proper development); the Underwater Fern known as *Ceratopteris thalictroides,* and the Madagascar Lace Plant.

Dealers supply many aquatic plants in the form of cuttings. They will root easily if you hold them securely in the gravel. You can wind lead wire around the lower end of the stem until sufficient weight has been added to anchor the cutting firmly in the sand. When plants have roots (for example, *Vallisneria*), clip the roots short and wind a small piece of lead wire around the plant directly above the root system.

After you have learned about the various types of plants that are available to you and have noted their characteristics, make a rough sketch of the plan and elevation of the aquarium as it will appear when it is ready for the fish. This will prevent haphazard planting and will save time and possible disappointment that will come if you have to move plants once they have rooted. As you make the sketches, you will think of other points for consideration (such as illumination during the hours of darkness).

PLANTING

After you have made your plan and acquired the plants you want you can begin planting them in the aquarium. First, wash all the plants thoroughly and examine them for such undesirable creatures as leeches, worms, snails, eggs, etc. Remove any object that is not part of the plant, such as the small red or black eggs frequently found tucked between new shoots of plants (the eggs of planarians), or immature forms of beetle larvae which may have become entangled in the roots. You may disinfect the new plants

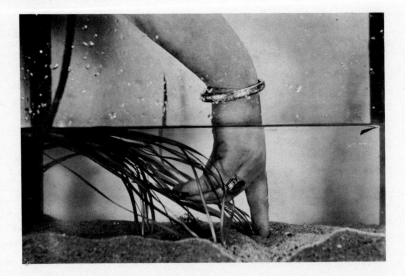

When you plant the aquarium, do not fill it with water or it will overflow when you put your hand into it. Use your extended index finger to poke ahead of the plant. If you shove the plant into the sand, you will surely break off the stem.

by leaving them for a few hours in a very weak solution of potassium permanganate (available at any pet shop). Add just enough to aged water at room temperature to turn it pinkish. If too much is used (and the water becomes purple) the plants will die or they will be damaged.

If the sand is already in the tank (as described on page 17) you can start planting. It is easier to plant in a few inches of water. So that you won't disturb the undulating surface of the sand, lay a sheet of paper in the tank and put a plate or saucer on it. If you pour the water onto the plate the level will gradually rise without disturbing the surface of the sand. It may be helpful to use plant sticks—thin pieces of wood notched at the ends. The sticks will thrust the roots of the plants well into the sand.

Plastic plants come in a variety of styles and sizes. Most plastic plants have cup-shaped bases designed to be buried in the gravel to prevent the plants from floating.

After you finish the planting, bring the water to its final level (approximately 1½ inches from the top) and let the tank settle for as long a time as your patience will allow—*but certainly for not less than three days.* You will notice many changes occurring during this period of establishment: many gas bubbles will cover the plants and glass and the water may tend to become a little cloudy. It will finally clear and when the tank is really settled it will have the clarity that a healthy aquarium should display. It is a mistake to change the water because of a little cloudiness (if you have properly washed the sand and taken the other necessary steps). The cloudiness will only reappear as the new water attempts to balance its population of microscopic life.

The Wakin is the common goldfish of Japan. It has short fins. The colors may be yellow, orange, white, or, as in this fish, a red-orange and white combination. Photo courtesy Midori Shobo, *Fish Magazine*, Japan.

Telescope-eyed goldfish such as this one are referred to as Demekin. The red one is an Aka Demekin. Photo courtesy Midori Shobo, *Fish Magazine*, Japan.

The Aka Demekin (also known as the red metallic globe-eye) starts to develop the telescope-eye at an age of about one month. If only one eye develops or the sizes are different, this constitutes a flaw. Photo courtesy Midori Shobo, *Fish Magazine*, Japan.

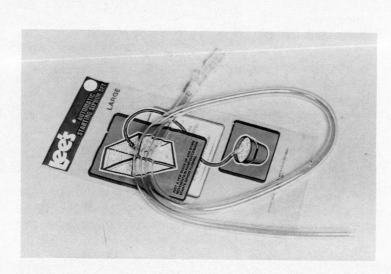

Siphon for removing water from aquarium without fuss or muss.

A pH kit, a device used for measuring the relative acidity or alkalinity of aquarium water. An abrupt change in the pH value of their water can kill goldfish, and it is wise to have one of these easy-to-use and inexpensive kits on hand at all times.

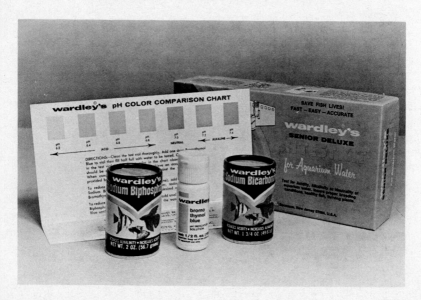

Some aquarium ornaments are strictly for decoration, but many can
be used as aerators as well.

Cabomba is a plant that is suitable for either the home aquarium
or the garden pool.

The celestial goldfish or Chotengan was apparently derived from the red telescope. Photo courtesy Midori Shobo, *Fish Magazine*, Japan.

The usual color of the celestial goldfish is orange-yellow as seen here. The eyes are normal in the very young fish, the change starting at about four months of age. Photo courtesy Midori Shobo, *Fish Magazine*, Japan.

The peacocktail (Jikin, Rokurin, Shachi, or Kujyaku) was developed from the Wakin. The most desirable type of peacocktail is the one shown above with the red lips and fins; it is called a Rokurin. The characteristic X-shaped tail is best seen in the photo below.

Photos courtesy Midori Shobo, *Fish Magazine*, Japan.

OXYGENATION

Much has been written about the value of supplying extra oxygen to aquatic plants in ornamental aquaria. Oxygenation for large aquaria is discussed below. First you should understand the process known as photosynthesis that is normal to all green plants. Photosynthesis is the ability of a green plant to convert carbon dioxide (the waste gas of animal life) into the carbohydrates required for its growth and metabolism. During this process the excess oxygen is released either into the atmosphere or into the water, depending on the type of plant. Some aquarium plants that are exposed to strong sunlight will give off a steady stream of very

Giant Vallisneria is only suitable for very deep tanks and for pools. It gives off plenty of oxygen when exposed to strong sunlight. It may grow to 6 feet in height.

small bubbles that apparently leave some pore or crack in a stem or leaf. This is pure oxygen. (You can see it pouring upward from the leaves of *Vallisneria* or *Elodea crispa* when the plants are in the sunlight.) In the absence of light, however, the process is reversed and carbon dioxide is given off while oxygen is absorbed.

The steady stream of oxygen that is released by aquatic plants may be beneficial to terrestrial animals, but fish can only use oxygen dissolved in water. Thus the oxygenation ability of aquarium plants is of little direct value to goldfish in an aquarium.

AERATORS AND FILTERS

Until now we have discussed the simplest form of aquarium, which is the most trouble-free and satisfactory for the beginner. We will now consider certain refinements that you may add to increase the number of fish kept in the tank.

The first refinement is a small aerator, usually a vibrator-type pump with rubber diaphragms. It will provide a steady stream of small bubbles that will rise from the porous air stone that is attached to the pump by rubber or plastic tubing and then placed on the bottom of the aquarium. (Rubber tubing should not be continually in contact with the water. To prevent this contact there are diffuser stones with plastic tubes of sufficient length to suit the depth of water. The best type of stone is one that provides a fine cloud of very small bubbles.) The purpose of the aerator is to ensure a uniform oxygen content in the water by means of rapid circulation. It is commonly but erroneously believed that the bubbles produced add oxygen to the water. They do not—they remove carbon dioxide gas dissolved in the water by a simple exchange. The bubbles also create a current that exposes fresh volumes of water to the atmosphere at the surface, bringing about a gaseous exchange with the air. If the entire surface of the water is covered by such floating aquatic plants as *Riccia, Salvinia* or Duckweed, the efficiency of this apparatus is greatly reduced.

The piston type of pump, though more expensive, is more reliable. This type is silent; some vibrator type pumps hum. A piston

The Tancho or redcap goldfish is a striking variety derived from the Kohaku. The ideal pattern is pure white with only a round red marking on the top center of the head. Photo courtesy Midori Shobo, *Fish Magazine*, Japan.

The calico oranda or Azumanishiki is seen in the photos above and below. It is a hardy variety and can grow as large as other orandas. It was developed by crossing orandas with the calico telescope-eyed goldfish. Photos courtesy Midori Shobo, *Fish Magazine*, Japan.

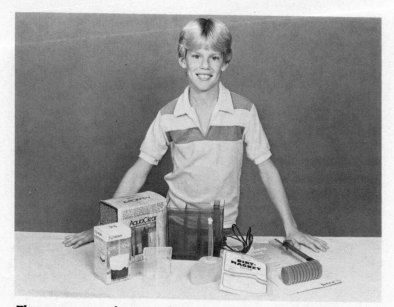

There are several types of filters available for your aquarium. Shown here are a corner filter, outside power filter, and sponge filters.

pump can be used in the same way as a vibrator pump or it can be attached to a filter as well. Air forced from the pump pushes water up a plastic tube to a filter box of one sort or another. The flow of air must be adjusted so that each bubble lifts its maximum amount of water. If the air flow is too fast, practically no water will be filtered; if it is too slow, the flow will be intermittent.

The filter box is usually a plastic container with a layer of bone charcoal on the bottom and glass wool on top of the charcoal. The filtering medium can be replaced once a week or as often as necessary. If the filter is housed inside the aquarium, the water slowly drips through, becoming thoroughly aerated as well as cleansed on its passage. If, however, an outside filter is used, a siphon must be arranged to deliver the water to the filter and the

Vibrator pumps require no maintenance and consume much less electric current than piston pumps. Small vibrator pumps are ideal for small tanks.

air lift must be placed in the filter so that filtered water can be returned to the aquarium. Although it is more bulky, an outside filter is more efficient than the inside type.

If you use one of the filtering and aerating methods, you can keep a greater number of fish, but you should not overdo it. If some mechanical breakdown occurs (and this can happen to even the best equipment), serious trouble may follow very quickly. But it is true that filtration is especially useful for goldfish, who are always turning over the mulm at the bottom of the aquarium in search of food. Without a filter the water tends to become cloudy.

A lionhead or Ranchu with a fully developed hood. A well-developed hood should have the appearance of a ripe raspberry. Photo courtesy Midori Shobo, *Fish Magazine*, Japan.

This Ranchu also has a well-developed hood. The hood quality seems to be dependent upon such factors as water quality, water temperature, and diet, but it should start to make its appearance at about four months of age. Photo courtesy Midori Shobo, *Fish Magazine*, Japan.

Above and below: Lionheads may develop bright colors, but apparently not so bright as the Wakins or Ryukins. Ranchus are usually a metallic gold as seen here.

Photos courtesy
Midori Shobo,
Fish Magazine,
Japan.

Diatomaceous earth filters can help to clear up a dirty tank very quickly. For most efficient operation, such filters should have the filter material changed when it begins to show signs of becoming clogged up.

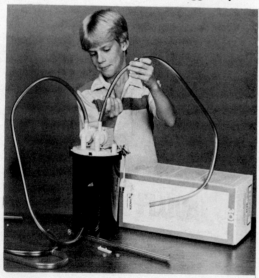

Canister filters should be used on large tanks. These filters circulate a great deal more water than the hanging outside filters. An additional benefit of the canister filter is that it can be placed in a cabinet several feet away from the aquarium.

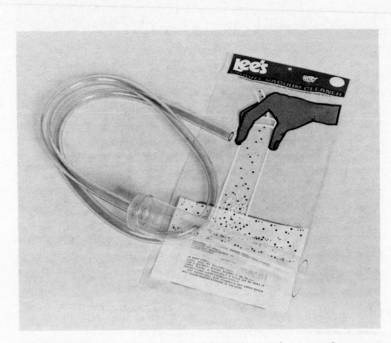

A gravel cleaner is a handy piece of equipment for removing excess food and wastes.

CLEANING THE AQUARIUM

If you are keeping the setup as simple as possible, it is necessary to remove the mulm and detritus when the accumulation becomes unattractive and the fish stir it up by swimming over it. You can do this quite quickly and simply with a 5-foot siphon tube and a bucket. After you siphon off the dirt, replace the amount of water removed with clean aged tap water of the same temperature as the water in the aquarium. (Add hot water to equalize the temperature.) Be sure that the goldfish do not come into contact with the end of the tube during the siphoning operation because the suction can injure them. Fish with protruding eyes are particularly liable to such injury.

The black telescope-eyed goldfish is more popularly known as the black moor; in Japan it is called the Kuro Demekin. The black pigment should become noticeable about two months after hatching. Photo courtesy Midori Shobo, *Fish Magazine*, Japan.

The black color of the black telescope-eyed oranda apparently is linked genetically with the telescope-eyed feature since the black only appears in the telescope-eyed variety. Photo courtesy Midori Shobo, *Fish Magazine*, Japan.

This is a Hageshiro koi. It is a Karasu Goi in which there are patches of white — here the snout and head have turned white. Photo courtesy Kodansha.

3. How to Choose Goldfish

After your aquarium is set up you are ready to get your gold-fish. If you are to have healthy fish, perhaps the most important factor is the way you select them. After you have experience, of course, a quick glance will immediately separate the fit from the ailing, but the beginner may not be able to recognize the symptoms of sickness.

Pick goldfish that move with extreme precision and with all fins alert and in use. If the fish is not physically damaged, has no missing scales, torn fins or signs of blood on body or fins, you will avoid initial trouble. A sick fish is a sad creature. Even in the first stages of disease it will have a drooping dorsal fin, closed ventral fins or it will move queerly.

You should know something about the outward appearance and internal organs and senses of goldfish. Then you will be able to choose undamaged fish and prevent later injury.

FINS

Look at the picture on page 53. The goldfish's fins are as follows: the dorsal or back fin, the caudal or tail fin, the anal fin and ventral fins around the vent, and the pectoral or breast fins just behind the gill openings. Goldfish do not have adipose fins. All these fins control movement; they do not start it. The movement of a fish is achieved by the alternating movement of muscles in the body wall. The fins merely modify the movement and give the desired direction and stability. You will notice that even when the goldfish seems motionless, the pectorals continue to move at intervals. This movement may bring a change of water, with renewed oxygen content, to the fish's head region.

Nasal
Oriface

Lateral
Line

Dorsal Fin

Caudal Fin

Gill
Plate

Pectoral
Fins

Ventral
Fins

Anal
Fin

Dorsal Fin

Lionhead

Caudal Fin

Gill
Plate

Pectoral
Fins

Anal
Fin

Ventral
Fins

The Kuchibeni Kohaku is given this name because of the red color on the lips, the name thus meaning the red-lipped Kohaku. Kohaku refers to the red and white color combination. Photo courtesy Kodansha.

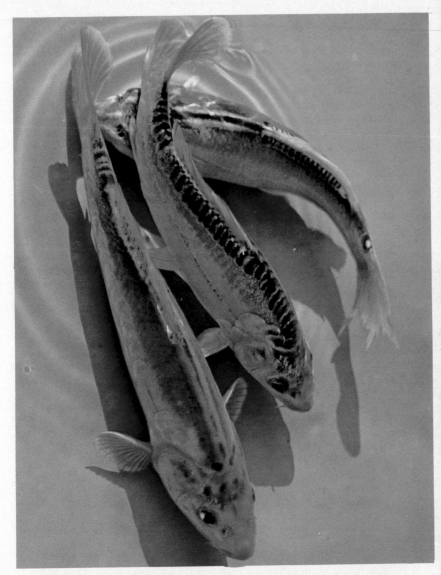

The green carp or Etsu No Hisoku was developed by crossing a female Shusui with a male Yamabuki Ohgon. The color is basically a yellowish green, the scales being a metallic golden or platinum. Photo courtesy Kodansha.

COLORS

Some goldfish are strongly colored blue, purple, orange or black. But you can see these colors at their best only if the fish are sufficiently protected from strong light. The color of a goldfish changes as its environment changes. If a wild carp is placed in a white bowl, its color will gradually recede until within twenty minutes the fish will have a pale, washed-out appearance. If it is then placed in a black bowl, its color will return to normal in about the same length of time. However, this color change will not take place on blind fish or on goldfish that cannot see their background. This is because the eye sets off nervous impulses that cause the color cells to contract or expand according to the light impulses received. You can see, then, that a fish kept continually over a light-colored gravel will not show as much intensity of color as it would if it had a darker background.

The goldfish is one of the most variable species of fish in existence. (See Chapter 4 for detailed descriptions of the varieties.) It was probably this characteristic that led to its culture by man.

Goldfish of the common type are dull bronze until they are several months old. Some remain this color for the rest of their lives but a large number, if they have enough sunlight and warmth and good food, slowly turn yellow-orange, silver or a combination of these colors. This change is caused by a gradual loss of the black pigment—a phenomenon known as xanthochroism. Therefore, it is of little value to choose young goldfish because they have some peculiarly shaped black markings, since these may completely disappear in a short time. (Some original markings may reappear as a result of injury or advancing age.)

SWIM BLADDERS

Internally, a goldfish has two small bladders filled with gas. These lie directly behind the head and above the gut. They are known as the swim bladders, and besides helping the goldfish to maintain its balance they act as an additional method of hearing

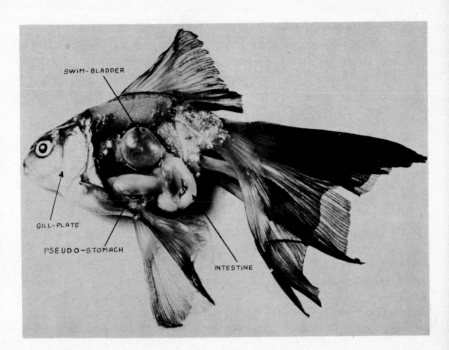

The internal organs of a goldfish.

through a complicated series of little bones known as the Weberian ossicles (named after their discoverer). But the swim bladders can be a nuisance to the fish, since any chilling is likely to affect them and cause severe imbalance in the body. A goldfish troubled with this will be unable to leave the bottom of the tank for any length of time.

TEETH

The teeth of goldfish are very small. They are arranged in two rows of four each and they bite against a hard pad that forms the upper palate. The number and arrangement of teeth, incidentally, are used to identify the different members of the carp family.

The Aka-Bekko is a beautiful koi in which the main color is red accented with black. The Aka-Bekko (red + black), Shiro-Bekko (white + black), and Ki-Bekko (yellow + black) are also known as the tortoise-shell koi. Photo courtesy Kodansha.

Opposite: The Purachina Kohaku or Kin Fuji is a platinum Ohgon with some red patches. Unfortunately the red color is very weak and detracts from its value. Photo courtesy Kodansha.

SCALES

Goldfish scales are large. There are 26 to 35 rows of scales from the gill opening to the beginning of the tail (the caudal peduncle). Observe that a line of scales in the middle of the side has little dots. These dots are really pits that make up the lateral line, a sense organ that makes the fish sensitive to low sounds and to temperature changes in the water. The exact functions of the lateral line are not fully known, but further study may provide other vital information about the fish's environment.

Three kinds of scales are found on various types of goldfish. The difference is caused by the amount of reflecting tissue on the back of the scales and behind them.

The first of the scale groups are often known as *scaled type* goldfish, but are badly named, since all goldfish have scales. A better name is *metallic-scaled*. This aptly describes the metallic luster on the common goldfish.

The second group also have a badly-chosen name. They are known as *calico* goldfish, presumably in an attempt to describe the mottled pattern so common to this type. A better name (coined by the Goldfish Society of Great Britain) is *nacreous* fish, for this describes the slight shine to the scales, through which show the many varied calico colors.

The last group, erroneously called *scaleless,* are perhaps better described as *matt* fish. Here there is no shine at all. The irridicytes, the crystal-like substance in the scales that produces the shine, are entirely absent so that the body appears transparent, especially with pale and flesh-colored specimens.

PIGMENTS

The last two groups can show varying shades of blue, sometimes combined with patches of deep red-orange, yellow, purple and black. The colors make a truly handsome fish.

There are only three color pigments in goldfish: orange, yellow and black. Any other color must be produced by combinations of these together with the refraction of light caused by the colors' depth in the body wall. The beautiful blues come from the black pigment which is dispersed in the body wall in such a way that it gives the appearance of blue.

The enormous difference in shape, fins and color among the many different types of goldfish is the result of careful selective breeding over the years. If different types are kept together, they will readily interbreed and produce worthless fish with a mixture of characteristics.

Above: Oranda goldfish with a dorsal fin and long flowing fins. **Below:** Lionhead goldfish without a dorsal and with short fins. The great variation among goldfish is what makes their breeding so interesting.

The Taisho-Sanshoku koi is a tricolored variety. The main color is white with accents of black and red. This individual was reported (in 1973) to have been the best Tancho in the world. Photo courtesy Kodansha.

Orandas come in many colors including red, red and white combined, orange-yellow, Crucian gray, and black. In China additional colors, including blue, blue-brown, and brown (the two shown here), have been developed. Photo courtesy Midori Shobo, *Fish Magazine*, Japan.

4. Goldfish Varieties

Although well over 100 varieties of goldfish are known and bred, here we will just discuss those that have reached Europe and America, since it is only those that we have had the opportunity to breed, study and record. Many varieties are only slightly different from those goldfish we know; others are rare (or perhaps are not recognized as separate varieties) and do not find their way to our markets.

The common goldfish (*Carassius auratus*), ancestor of all the others, is recognized in only one form: metallic-scaled and short-finned. For show purposes it should have a good, uniform red color, although some are yellow, orange, silver or combinations of these colors mixed with black patches. The dorsal and ventral elevation (see illustration on page 53) should have a smooth curved contour. (Poor specimens develop a snout which completely spoils this line.) The head should be small and the fins broad and short.

If your goldfish are for decorative purposes only, you may prefer other colors. Remember that any black markings will eventually fade away. Goldfish usually lose these markings in three or four months, although sometimes the change takes much longer. Parti-colored fish (red and silver, and so forth) usually retain their markings, although the silver may spread (because of the elimination of the orange pigment) until the fish appear completely white.

Do not purchase any of the metallic types that do not clearly show the color change. Although all metallic goldfish are bronze for the early part of their lives, they do not all color, but some remain the dull greenish-bronze of the wild fish.

Crucian Carp (*Carassius carassius*), a near relative of the goldfish, can easily be mistaken for an uncolored goldfish. This is particularly apt to occur with the variety of the Crucian Carp known as the Prussian Carp. However, there are differences between goldfish and Crucian Carp that you can see. Goldfish have larger scales, 26 to 35 along the lateral line and from 4 to 6 from the beginning of the dorsal fin to the lateral line. Crucian Carp have from 28 to 35 scales in the lateral line and from 7 to 9 from the beginning of the dorsal fin to the lateral line. The dorsal fin of the goldfish presents a straight or slightly concave outside edge; the fin margin of the Crucian Carp is convex, with the fin rays increasing in length toward the center of the fin. Again, the Prussian Carp superficially resembles the ordinary goldfish more closely because its body is not much wider. If you plan to breed your goldfish, you should be able to tell them from Carp to prevent interbreeding.

SCALE GROUPS

Each variety of goldfish may be obtained in the three different scale groups—metallic, nacreous and matt (see page 60), although the division may seem rather arbitrary. There are some types in varying stages from completely metallic to almost translucent (matt). The best specimens of the nacreous group (also known as calico fish) are those which exhibit few or no areas of metallic luster. (Points are deducted from show fish with any shiny scales or "hard" metallic gill-plates.) They usually have a dull sheen that comes from scattered irridicytes deep in the body wall. These irridicytes, common to most fish, cause the silvery whiteness that so many exhibit. They are crystal deposits of a substance known as guanin, a waste product of the blood. In fish, which have a poor excretory system compared to higher animals, these waste products are carried to the skin and to places where they can do no harm.

Thus the silver coloration of goldfish is structural. The other colors—orange, yellow or black—are true pigments that are contained in little sac-like cells. The pigment may contract or expand to increase or decrease the particular color. (This mechanism is triggered by the fish's eyesight when it becomes aware of any drastic difference between its color and its surroundings. Blind fish are not capable of protective coloration—changing color to blend with their surroundings. Any change of color brought about this

The basic species from which the common and fancy varieties of goldfish were derived is *Carassius auratus*, seen here as very unspectacular fish.

A young comet goldfish. The black markings on the fins and body will eventually disappear, making the entire fish orange. Photo by Andre Roth.

The comet is one of the more common varieties of goldfish and was developed in the United States around 1880. It is hardy and prolific and is well suited to outdoor pools. Photo by Andre Roth.

way is temporary. Many experiments with fish have shown that their ability to change color improves with practice.)

In the three types of fish recognized by goldfish enthusiasts the guanin content is normal, completely absent or very thinly scattered. During the crossbreeding of these types, certain interesting facts come to light. If two nacreous fish are bred, 50% of the offspring will be nacreous, 25% metallic and 25% matt. If metallic is crossed with matt, the young will all be nacreous. Matt crossed with nacreous will yield 50% of each; similarly, metallic crossed with nacreous will yield 50% of each type. Finally, if metallic is mated to metallic or matt to matt, the fry will all resemble the parents. These figures show that Mendelian processes are at work and that the various types are genetically divided. Many other factors are involved (such as inhibitor genes) and the whole subject of color and scaling has many problems.

FANCY VARIETIES

THE COMET GOLDFISH is a very handsome type. It is streamlined, with much larger fins than the common variety. The tail is deeply forked and is often as long as, if not longer than, the body. In the early 1950's Comets were reasonably plentiful, but good specimens are now very difficult to obtain. The usual coloration is completely primrose yellow or red. Parti-colored specimens have less value. They do not usually exceed eight inches in over-all length. *Comets for show purposes must be metallic.* These fish are difficult to breed in aquariums, since they are very active and require more space. They should be bred in small pools.

SHUBUNKINS are usually thought of as nacreous and matt, because the word Shubunkin has become synonymous with the handsome blue and mottled specimens with which this type was introduced. (They will produce a percentage of metallics and matts when bred.) It is only possible to obtain the rich blue coloration if the scales are not completely masked by the metallic gleam. Remember that there is no blue pigment in goldfish. The beautiful blues are the result of the refraction of light from black pigment deep in the body wall. Blue, then, is visible only if the layers of irridicytes are absent or greatly diffused.

Two types of Shubunkin are recognized. The *London Shubunkin* has short fins and, except for color, looks like the common goldfish. The *Bristol Shubunkin* is a handsome variety with well-developed broad finnage. The caudal fin is very large and rounded. These fish make fine aquarium specimens and their color is always attractive. They can be bred in small aquaria (24 x 12 x 12).

A young red metallic fantail goldfish.

A 4-year-old male Comet goldfish. The plants in the background are Hornwort (left) and *Vallisneria*.

Opposite page, top:
The fantail goldfish with double caudal and anal fins is the first major deviation from the normal goldfish shape. This one shows good body shape and fin development. Photo by Andre Roth.

Opposite page, bottom: A 4-year-old male Bristol Shubunkin. It has longer finnage than the London Shubunkin.

THE FANTAIL exhibits the first great deviation from the normal goldfish shape. It seems to have two tails set so that the lower lobes of each are much further apart than the upper ones. In good specimens, the anal fin should be double. The twin tails and anals are caused by a division of the original single fin, a fact which you may verify by looking at a number of fantail youngsters. As young fantails develop many will show different stages in this process of division while some, though of normal double-tailed parents, will have single tails. It is quite common to find youngsters with tails that have a single top lobe and a double bottom lobe, or vice versa. These are generally known as tri-tailed or web-tailed. They are worthless for show purposes. This characteristic is quite usual with all the twin-tailed varieties, as they have a strong tendency to revert to the original single-tail formation.

Fantails are recognized in all scale groups but the most prized are red metallics. Red metallics are exceptionally hardy fish with truer characteristics than the nacreous or matt types, which are often not truebred but throwouts from such longer tailed varieties as the veiltail. A good fantail should have an egg-shaped body, small head and short pointed finnage. The tail should be carried very stiffly. Fantails are very desirable for the decorative aquarium.

THE VEILTAIL is considered the most beautiful of all the goldfish varieties. The graceful movements of this fish are like those of a ballerina. However, the veiltail presents problems. You will see in the illustrations that the finnage in a veiltail goldfish is excessive and the body is almost spherical. These deviations from the normal shape cause various difficulties for the fish itself and complicate its care.

First of all, there is the question of equilibrium. Goldfish, you know, have swim bladders, air sacs that affect the specific gravity of the fish (act as a hydrostatic organ) and serve as an additional method of hearing. It is believed that the swim bladders also enable communicative sounds to be passed. As the rotund body develops, there are certain changes in the size and location of these bladders. It is not uncommon for veiltails to become unbalanced as they reach maturity. This organ appears to be very sensitive to chill—even ordinary goldfish are likely to become unbalanced if they are subjected to too great a change in temperature. In veiltails the swim bladder is especially delicate.

The long fins can be easily damaged by careless handling or improper feeding, both of which can cause the marginal areas of the caudal, and possibly the ventrals, to become bloodshot and ragged. With proper care and plenty of live food veiltails should live about ten years, and there are cases on record where they have lived much longer.

The most popular form of veiltail is the calico or nacreous type that has the mottled coloration of the Shubunkin, preferably on a

A young telescope-eyed veiltail goldfish.

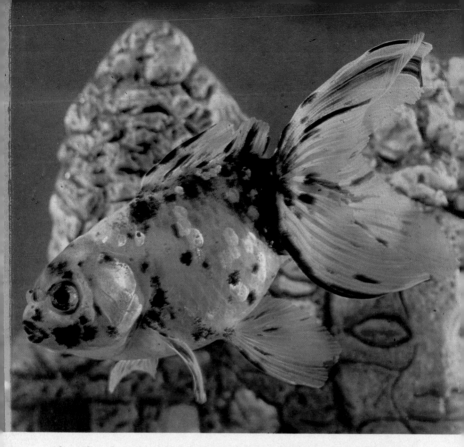

The calico fantail goldfish is derived from crossings of red fantails with calico telescopes.

Opposite page, top: A beautiful all-white fringe tail goldfish. Photo courtesy Midori Shobo, *Fish Magazine*, Japan.

Opposite page, bottom: From left to right, a male metallic veiltail, a male matt veiltail and a female calico veiltail, all from the same spawning of two calico parents. There may be a great variation between brother and sister in any spawning.

background of blue. But the color of these fish is seldom as brilliant as that of the Shubunkin. There are some metallic types but the only early-coloring metallics are those that have been imported from Japan or China. (Their scarcity may be related to the color selection necessary for the calico types.) Imported Oriental fish have body shapes and finnage different from that found acceptable to American or British goldfish societies.

Occasionally metallic offspring from the calico types do color. When this occurs, it is usually a rather slow process, taking about two to three years.

There are several standards for the veiltail. A specimen is generally expected to have fully divided caudals, as long or longer than the body, twin anals and an almost spherical body. The dorsal fin should be as high as the body is deep and held erect. A good red color in the metallics is preferred to the yellow usually seen. At least one society is aiming at parti-colored specimens.

THE TELESCOPE-EYED VEILTAIL is another type of veiltail with protruding eyes. Its only difference is its eyes. They are enlarged to great globes which protrude as much as one-half to three-quarters of an inch from the head. These fish have exceedingly poor eyesight because of the malformation of the eye and its lens. They are best kept in their own aquarium. Since the eye is easily damaged there should be no rough surfaces left exposed in the aquarium. The telescope-eyed veiltail is often produced when attempts are made to breed the Moor.

THE MOOR is the only black goldfish known, although occasionally other types (lionheads, celestials, etc.) do show this coloration for short periods of time. In shape and finnage the Moor resembles the telescope-eyed veiltail, but the velvet-black specimens are of the metallic type. The intense black color is in some way related to the protruding eye. So far it has been impossible to produce any normal-eyed black goldfish. Many specimens of the Moor change color as they age. Often a bronziness on the under-surface is an indication of the color change to come. Really good Moor specimens command a high price and are rather rare.

A head-on view of a telescope-eyed veiltail goldfish.

A veiltail goldfish with protruding eyes is called a telescope-eyed veiltail. Shown here are two red telescope-eyed goldfish. Photo courtesy Midori Shobo, *Fish Magazine*, Japan.

Opposite page, top: Two 1-year-old pearl scale goldfish. A calico variety is on the left and a metallic on the right. It will take at least another year for their scales to become fully distended.

Opposite page, bottom: An 18-month-old pearl scale undergoing a color change.

A veiltail Moor, showing an excellent example of a fully divided tail fin (caudal)

A young Moor is quite bronze with normal eyes. The change to the black coloration and the bulging of the eyes begins about ten or twelve weeks after hatching. At this age it is comparatively short-finned and resembles an uncolored fantail. Only experience can help you pick those specimens that are likely to develop into robust adults with flowing fins. Among a spawning of fish, those which appear undersized, yet have enormous finnage, are unlikely to carry out their early promise. They seldom reach maturity. (Many long-finned goldfish do not live long.) When you purchase fry, select the most robust specimens with good broad finnage and fully divided caudals and anals. Well-developed anals are about the best guide to whether the caudals will qualify for the expression "veiltail." This goldfish variety is known as the veiltail Moor.

A fantail variety of this breed is quite popular but it does not compare with the veiltail type for elegance and bizarre beauty.

THE PEARL SCALE is another variety of fantail, a comparatively new arrival from China. It is a grotesque fish with a bloated appearance (somewhat like a fish with dropsy). This is because of the formation of the scales, which have a small raised encrustation in the center that gives them a domed appearance. In the young pearl scale, small bladders that apparently contain fluid frequently appear where the pectorals join the body. These later

A fully developed pearl scale veiltail.

disappear, and little is known about their function or cause. Pearl-scaling sometimes appears on other varieties. These bladders are present when this occurs, so it is probable that they are connected with the secretory system concerned with the scaling.

There are several distinct breeds of goldfish in which the dorsal fin has been bred out. This fin is the most effective stabilizer that a fish has and its removal renders the fish less precise in its movements, especially if speed is attempted.

Pearl scaling is caused by the scales having a domed appearance, giving the fish a "dropsical" look. Shown is a pearl scale goldfish. Photo courtesy Midori Shobo, *Fish Magazine*, Japan.

The celestial goldfish is so named for the upturned eyes. The limited vision puts them at a disadvantage with the more active varieties, but alone they do very well. Photo by Andre Roth.

THE CELESTIAL, a very rare variety, is perhaps the most spectacular of the dorsal-less types. It is a grotesque creature with curious upturned eyes. Because of the position of their eyes, the fish cannot see anything at their sides or below them. In their quest for food, then, they must rely upon their sense of smell. But celestials are active goldfish and they can secure their share of food. However, it is not advisable to keep celestials with other types.

Although it is possible to breed celestials in the three scale groups, most of the specimens are metallic, either deep orange, yellow, or red and silver. There are many interesting stories of

83

The eyes of the celestial goldfish just about look at each other. This is the only animal known to science that is capable of staring into its own eyes. It cannot see anything that happens underneath its mouth. It takes almost one year for the eyes to turn fully upward.

their development. One story suggests that they were first bred in a Korean temple and considered holy fish since they gazed heavenward. Another suggests that the eye formation was first caused by keeping the young in darkened tanks with only a narrow slit of light at the top. This is not possible, since physical changes in animals cannot be brought about purely by environmental conditions.

It is known that celestials were first in evidence during the 18th century. For various reasons they never became plentiful.

THE WATER BUBBLE-EYE, somewhat similar to the celestial, has eyes that retain their normal position. A swelling beneath the eyes is filled with a thick fluid. This swelling can reach amazing proportions. When it does, the bladders are often deflated by damage. Even if the damage is not too serious, it takes many weeks to repair.

Thomas Horeman's water bubble-eye in a head-on view. This fish cannot see in front of itself, and is hardly considered beautiful.

Water bubble-eye goldfish are similar to the celestials, but the eye is in its normal position and there is a large sac below it that fills with a thick fluid. Photo courtesy Midori Shobo, *Fish Magazine*, Japan.

These fish are usually of the metallic type, mostly yellow or pale orange. The water bubble-eye is a new arrival from China. So far it has proved to be a robust and hardy variety, but it can hardly be termed beautiful. The young produced from time to time indicate that there has been a certain amount of crossing with the celestial. It is not uncommon to find celestials with partial fluid-filled bladders, and there is a decided upturn to the eyes of some of the water bubble-eye young.

The lionhead may go under several different names including bramble-head, Ranchu, and Shu Tze Tou. The head growth is developed with age and may become quite extensive. Photo courtesy Midori Shobo, *Fish Magazine*, Japan.

THE LIONHEAD is an old favorite. It presents a very odd appearance but it does not offend anyone's aesthetic sense, as the bubble-eye and celestial are likely to do. The lionhead is chubby, with a very arched back and no dorsal fin. The tail is of the fantail variety (small and stiffly held). It is the head, however, that distinguishes the fish. In good specimens the head is most peculiar, with a swollen pimply appearance that has been likened to a raspberry. This cranial growth is not seen in young specimens, but usually develops slowly and reaches maximum proportions in four to five years. At that time large areas of it may be shed. This queer growth of surface cells is similar to the secondary sexual characteristics of goldfish. The males usually produce a far better "hood" (as it is called) than do the females. The growth can be so heavy (especially when it covers the gill-plates) that breathing is impaired.

An Oranda goldfish is a lionhead with a dorsal fin. This fish, owned by Mr. Horeman, is fully hooded.

For this reason the breed should have more than average tank space unless some form of aeration is continually in action.

The lionhead is nearly always of the metallic type. The usual colors are deep orange, red and silver, and yellow. Sometimes the body is a peculiar brass color and the head is red.

THE ORANDA is a handsome fish, similar to the veiltail. It also has the cranial growth. Here the growth is usually confined to the interorbital space and does not often extend over the gill-plates and beneath the eyes as in the lionhead. This variety has a dorsal fin. The Oranda is only recognized in the metallic forms although many calico veils exhibit this growth as they grow old. This may be due to the unwise crossing of types. The usual color of the Oranda is bright orange but there are also red specimens.

A young male Oranda goldfish.

The oranda is similar to the lionhead but possesses a dorsal fin. In some orandas the head growth is limited to the area between the eyes, as in this calico oranda, but in most cases this may be only the most developed area. Photo courtesy Midori Shobo, *Fish Magazine*, Japan.

This oranda has a head growth much like that of the lionhead, but it is usually not as pronounced and develops at a later stage. Photo courtesy Midori Shobo, *Fish Magazine*, Japan.

The classic Chinese narial bouquet or pompon. The Chinese name bestowed upon this variety translates to "Dragon playing with red velvet ball." Photo courtesy Midori Shobo, *Fish Magazine*, Japan.

THE POMPOM is usually similar in body shape to the lion-head. Its nasal septum is overdeveloped and greatly enlarged to form what are frequently termed "narial bouquets." In other ways the head is that of a normal fish. In those specimens that have an excessive nasal growth, the growth is sucked into the mouth as the fish breathe. It is not a pretty sight at all. However, the average specimen is quite a perky little fish that has become very popular and has proved itself hardy and robust. About half the pompoms lack the dorsal fin, while half have it. Some pompoms look very much like the ordinary fantail goldfish except for the narial bouquet.

It would appear that the Chinese have developed this characteristic in two separate types of fish. It is difficult to maintain a dorsal-less condition, and throwbacks would be more likely to possess deformed dorsals or spines than the well-developed fins seen on these fish. After the distinct characteristic developed in

Mr. Horeman's pompom goldfish.

Compare this pompom (also owned by Mr. Horeman) with the illustration on the opposite page. Note the long caudal peduncle, the area between the tail fin and the anal region.

one type, it was probably extended by selection over a period of time to cover the two types.

Among the various forms of goldfish, some have a type of scale that has aroused considerable interest in goldfish circles. The effect is called "hammer-scaled" to describe the indented appearance. It is probable that this is an existing variety of goldfish in China, although it is not definitely known. Efforts are being made to develop a single-tailed hammer-scaled goldfish, but it will take considerable time to produce any appreciable results. However, the fish which do appear among spawnings from time to time are worthy specimens for the show aquarium since the feature is sufficiently striking to attract attention.

Selective goldfish breeding has achieved a great deal when full advantage has been taken of this very variable species. Of course, reversion is always rapid if the fish are left to breed under wild conditions and interbreeding can, and does, ruin many strains. However, the Chinese have apparently found it possible to maintain the types they have fixed by selective inbreeding and meticulous care.

5. How to Breed Goldfish

Of course before you can breed goldfish to plan you must be able to tell the difference between the sexes. Surprising as it may seem, old hands at the hobby occasionally make mistakes—even with adult specimens. It is almost impossible to tell the sex of fish six months of age or under, although the more precocious ones may show sufficient signs to permit a good guess.

The Nankin Ranchu or Nankin lionhead. Nankins have a color pattern called "Rokurin," with a white body and red on all fins, the gill cover, and the tip of the mouth. Photo courtesy Midori Shobo, *Fish Magazine*, Japan.

This rather oddly shaped goldfish is called a fringe tail. Photo courtesy Midori Shobo, *Fish Magazine*, Japan.

MALE-FEMALE DIFFERENCES

The signs are usually pretty unmistakable in mature fish during the spring breeding season. The male has raised tubercles (pimples) on the gill-plate and on the leading rays of the pectoral fins. These rough surfaces are used to excite the female when pre-spawning courting and the violent chase take place. (Courting among many goldfish is sometimes termed a "fish circus.")

The female in breeding season usually appears stouter on one side than the other. This is more noticeable in the elongated type of goldfish than in the very rotund type. Most females do not have tubercles but there are exceptions. Sometimes—though rarely—females show as many tubercles as any male; on the other hand—

and this is more common—some males never have tubercles. It is unlikely that you will come upon these oddities, but you should be aware of them.

Some people watch fish during the breeding season and select as males those fish that start a chase. This can be unreliable. If there are no male fish present, female fish may start the chase to rid themselves of the burden of ripe ova. There may also be a chase among male fish without females.

Many aquarists buy breeding trios consisting of two males and a female, but it is better to buy a half-dozen youngsters and select the breeders as they mature. It is almost a certainty that at least two pairs exist in any random selection of six young goldfish.

You may hear that a certain person has bred this or that fish. But this is nonsense—*the fish breed themselves*. Whether or not they breed is entirely dependent upon their state of health and the general conditions under which they are kept. Goldfish, especially in aquaria, will only breed if they are fit and not overcrowded. Lowering the temperature some four or five degrees (if the water is already 65° F. or more) may encourage breeding, but the health of the fish is the most important factor.

THE PRE-SPAWNING CHASE

Breeding will usually begin with a preliminary halfhearted chase. When you notice this, make sure the aquarium is well planted at both ends with bunches of suitable spawning plants, such as Hornwort, Milfoil, *Elodea crispa* or *Elodea canadensis*. Sometimes bunches of sterilized Spanish moss or a clump of nylon fibers will do just as well. If the female has spawned before, she will know exactly what to do. If it is the first time, she will dash blindly around the tank until, after much exertion, she eventually seems to realize that contact with the plants and the ensuing struggle against them brings relief. Be positive that the tank has no rocks or rough surfaces.

If your fish are in a pool, cover any rough edges in shallow places with plants. In newly constructed concrete pools where the

Oranda goldfish

surface has not had time to become covered with protective algae, females have had most of the scales dislodged from the ventral surface and sides. Their fins have also shown signs of severe cuts. Such fish will usually recover, grow new scales and repair the damage to fins, but it is senseless to allow such injuries to occur when they can so easily be prevented.

FERTILIZATION

The actual fertilization of the eggs takes place outside the female, since there is no physical connection between the sexes. This is what occurs. After a wild chase the female will dash into a bank of weeds and, by a violent flapping movement, spray some of her eggs. The male or males will follow as closely as possible, also flapping violently. While this flapping is going on, the male often presses his gill-plates hard against the head or abdomen of the female.

The eggs at first are very small, smaller than a grain of sugar, but they quickly swell by absorbing water to double their size. This swelling sometimes occurs within 10 seconds after spawning; they may swell a little after this but the greatest absorption of water occurs very rapidly. While the egg is absorbing water and swelling, sperm that is shed as the male gives off milt (the reproductive secretion) is drawn into the egg through a tiny opening known as the micropyle. Thus fertilization takes place.

CONDITIONING FISH FOR BREEDING

Getting fish into breeding condition is largely a matter of feeding. A good steady diet of garden worms at the right time (judged by temperature rather than by the calendar) is usually successful. Springtime, with its higher temperatures, is an ideal time to spawn goldfish. Goldfish can be stimulated by nearly any five- to ten-degree temperature rise, at any time of the year.

A method that never fails with healthy fish involves feeding about a cupful of bloodworms (*Chironomus* larvae) to the chosen pair or trio. One feeding will usually be enough but it can be repeated for several days if necessary. The only difficulty may be getting enough bloodworms.

HOW TO GET BLOODWORMS

Bloodworms are the larvae of the *Chironomus* fly, which looks like the ordinary gnat or mosquito but does not bite. The female fly may lay many capsules of eggs in a small pan of water containing rotten leaves. Usually a garden rain barrel contains many *Chironomus* larvae together with other suitable forms of goldfish food such as mosquito larvae and Cyclops. The egg capsule of the *Chironomus* is transparent and sausage-shaped. It is about one-half to three-quarters of an inch long and jelly-like. What looks like a coiled spring runs along its length. The eggs are usually attached to the side of the container at water level. Be careful not to dislodge or disturb them as each egg contains hundreds of potential larvae.

Full-grown *Chironomus* larvae, or bloodworms, are brilliant scarlet and about three-quarters of an inch in length. They live in a small tube made of detritus, which is attached to dead leaves, or the side of the barrel, or the surface of other objects at the bottom of the water. If you shake the barrel to dislodge them they will swim into open water. They move in the water by rapidly doubling their bodies backwards and forwards in a looping figure-eight fashion.

HOW TO MAKE A NET

You can net them in water with a fine mesh net made from the top of an old nylon stocking. This is how to make the net. First cut off and discard the foot of the stocking. Then make a small hole at the top edge where the nylon is double. Thread a piece of soft wire through the hole and bend it to form a firm ring lying inside the double material. Twist the free end to form a handle. Then tie a knot above any holes or runs the stocking may already have. This piece of apparatus will last for months and is useful for capturing all kinds of aquatic fish food. Make another one when it is worn out.

BREEDING TANK

After you have conditioned the goldfish with proper feeding, you can prepare for the eventual spawning. Since goldfish devour their eggs, you should provide a separate container for the bunches of plants to which the eggs will adhere. A shallow pan or aquarium will do. It must have a good surface area. The plants holding the ova must have enough room for each frond to receive proper light and air. Otherwise parts of the plants may quickly die and rot. They will then foul the water and the eggs or fry will die.

The water that will contain the eggs should be between 70° and 75° F. so that the fry can develop and hatch in approximately four days. Higher temperatures may speed up the hatching time to as little as 2½ to 3 days, while lower temperatures will extend the time to as much as 14 days and expose the ova to greater risk.

STERILIZATION

Fry are frequently attacked by a very small trematode (parasite worm) known as a fluke. It is advisable to sterilize the parents before spawning them, since nearly all goldfish carry their quota of this parasite.

Most fish that are bred in large ponds escape this fluke plague because the rapidly multiplying flukes are not confined with the fish in a small volume of water.

There are two kinds of fish flukes: *Gyrodactylus* and *Dactylogyrus*. The former multiply by dropping eggs which become free-swimming when they hatch and attach themselves to the first fish available. The latter type of fluke is live-bearing and much more difficult to get rid of. Flukes do little damage to grown fish unless the fish become completely infected. This rarely occurs in clean surroundings. However, they are very dangerous to fry and should not be present.

The presence of these parasites is indicated by the fish's behavior. It will dash wildly around, knocking itself against the plants or stones in an effort to free itself of an irritation. When the gills are infested, the breathing of the fish may be seriously impaired; no matter how fresh the water is, the fish will still mouth at the surface. Since most fish do carry this parasite, at the first sign of infestation you should clean the aquarium completely and sterilize the fish.

One sterilization method is to keep the fish in a salt bath for a few days, changing the solution daily. Two tablespoonsful of aquarium salt to the gallon of water is about the right strength. A chemical bath may affect individual fish differently, for their tolerance varies greatly. Watch each goldfish. If any show signs of acute distress, weaken the solution, but don't use it again until the fish have had a chance to recover from the shock of too strong a salt bath.

Another method of sterilizing the fish is to leave them for 24 hours in a very weak solution of potassium permanganate—0.01 grams per gallon of water. Repeat this bath every other day until the fish have had three doses. This sterilizing process, if not done properly, may have a very weakening effect upon the fish, so if you have any doubts, omit it.

You may use both methods alternately.

HANDSPAWNING

Handspawning can be very useful, but most accounts of the subject are either misleading or wrong. Whether you handspawn goldfish or allow them to breed naturally, they must be very healthy.

The ova may be taken from a female only when she is spawning or is prepared to spawn; any attempt before this causes injury or death to the fish. If the ova were extracted by cutting the fish open, they would be valueless. The eggs have to pass through a maturation period before they are laid; ova not properly mature cannot be fertilized.

If you want to handspawn, wait until the fish is in the process of laying the eggs, or until the activity going on and her condition indicate that she is ready. Then carefully lift her from the water. If she is ready, her slightest struggle will spray a few eggs onto your hand. If the males have also shown by chasing her that they are fit, you may begin handspawning.

Net the breeding fish and place them in a small container where they will be ready for the next step. Then fill a small bowl with

101

This is the proper way to hold a male goldfish. The illustration shows the pan and the exact place where you should apply pressure so you don't injure the fish.

water from the tank in which the fish were spawning. Add suitable fine-leaved water plants that conceal the entire bottom and sides of the bowl. It does not matter if the plants seem closely packed as you will move them to the breeding tank later. Take the male fish from the waiting container and hold it half under the water in the bowl, applying slight pressure a little above and in front of the anal pore. If the fish is ripe, a small puff of white milt will drift into the water. This single spray will be more than sufficient. Do not try to obtain as much as possible; it is pointless and you may rupture the fish. Return the fish to his bowl. Slightly stir the water

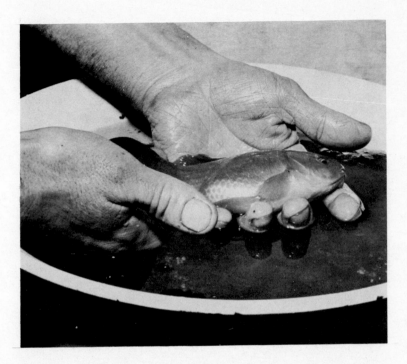

Hold the female goldfish this way. Note her distended abdomen swollen with ova. If she is ripe, the eggs will squirt out just from her movements and the pressure of the hand.

containing the plants and milt so that the milt spreads to all parts of the water.

Then net the female, and, holding her gently, move her around the bowl half in and half out of the water. Her occasional struggles will scatter ova in such a way that the eggs will be spread around fairly evenly. These eggs, as they fall through the water, will adhere to the first piece of plant they touch. If you are not careful, many eggs will fall in the same spot and stick together. You will have great difficulty in separating them later and they will not receive proper aeration and will eventually become covered with fungus.

Celestial goldfish.

Do not competely strip the female. You will have more than enough ova by the time she has struggled two or three times.

Do not allow the bowl containing the milt and eggs to stand for more than a half-hour, if at all, or the eggs might jell together and become inseparable. It is vital that you drain off all the water reasonably soon and gently wash the plants and ova with fresh water of the same temperature. Then place the plants in the aquarium prepared for them. Spread them out so that they receive adequate light. If the weather is very cold it may be necessary to add a small thermostatically controlled aquarium heater. But normally it should be warm enough during the breeding season, especially if the aquarium is indoors.

Twenty-four hours later examine the ova and see if your attempt has been as successful as it should be. Infertile eggs will be white, while fertilized eggs will be amber and clear and difficult to see. This will be more marked the following day, and it will be very difficult to see the fertile ova because of their transparence. Even when the embryonic fish is well developed inside the egg, it is hard to see. If you see only white eggs, don't think your spawning attempt was a failure. Carefully lift the plants, a stalk at a time, and hold them to the light. Any fertile eggs will immediately glisten.

Handspawning usually results in a high percentage of fertility—about 90% or more. It is useful for other reasons too. Goldfish usually take quite a few hours to complete a natural spawning. If you observe spawning activity when you arise in the morning, you can finish the process by handspawning in 15 minutes and leave the house knowing that the eggs will not be devoured by hungry

Goldfish eggs.

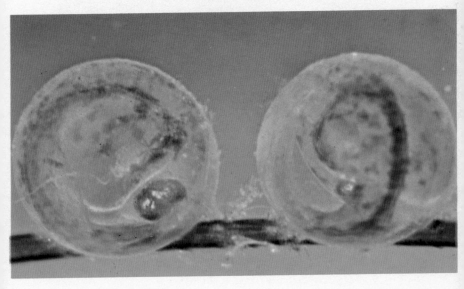

Newly hatched goldfish fry attached to the front glass of the aquarium.

parents. Handspawning is also useful if you have a lazy male or a short-sighted male who may not be able to locate the female. Again, if one of the pair is vicious, or if you intend to make a special cross, handspawning can be useful.

NATURAL BREEDING

If you intend to allow your goldfish to breed naturally, you will probably use the community method, placing all the males and females of the same variety together in a large aquarium. Cover the entire bottom of the breeding aquarium with artificial spawning grass (Spanish moss), or a dense batch of fine-leaved plants.

Place the breeders in and raise the temperature of the water five to ten degrees. Change about 25% of the water to fresh water of the same temperature. Usually water right from the tap will be all right if it doesn't contain too much chlorine. Within a few days, if the goldfish are in proper breeding condition, the group should show signs of spawning activity. Notice those fish that participate in the circus and remove all the others as they will only follow the breeders as they spawn and eat the eggs.

Remove all fish after spawning and allow the ova to hatch alone.

Do not crossbreed fish of different varieties. It is very difficult to produce good specimens even from truebred stock. It has taken years, patience and experience to establish these types, and mongrels which outwardly appear to be a specified type can greatly disappoint anyone who unwittingly uses them with good stock.

After your fish have spawned, give them the same conditioning food to get them into breeding condition again. This will take a little longer with the females than with the males. If the males begin chasing a reluctant female with spawning vigor, remove them or the female to prevent damage.

Under ideal conditions fish will spawn up to a half-dozen times in a season. However, since as many as 5,000 eggs are laid at a spawning (according to the size of the fish) you can see that one good spawning of a variety is ample for non-commercial goldfish breeders. Quality rather than quantity is what counts for the intelligent breeder.

If you are breeding any of the fancy varieties and want quality fish, take care in selecting the parents. Discard any breeders that show some marked fault, such as a turned-up snout, a body that is long where it should be round, a tail that is webbed or otherwise faulty instead of divided. Such faults in the parents will affect the quality of the fry. Even those fry that appear good will probably prove useless when they breed. Their fry will show a greater percentage of faults than the parents did.

(You can dispose of the faulty goldfish very economically by selling them to your local pet shop dealer. He will, in turn, offer them to the not-so-serious goldfish enthusiast who is more interested in general beauty than specific details.)

Of course, it is not always possible to have perfect specimens for breeding. In fact, it is seldom possible, but you should choose fish with only minor faults. For example, if a fish has one anal fin where two should exist, it is not very serious. In a breeder, smaller finnage is preferable to long finnage that is deeply forked instead of straight (as in the veiltail), or to pointed finnage that should be rounded (as in the Shubunkin). You will learn more by experience than by any reading, of course.

Naturally you should not use any specimens that show a marked weakness, such as imbalance or a tendency to have some recurring complaint. In fact, if you plan to do serious breeding it is best if you discard faulty fish at once. Finally, if you are keeping many fish, try to keep a written record of everything concerned with breeding. Memory is not reliable, especially when you are trying to establish a new strain. Remember this: it takes just as much time and effort to raise poor quality fish as it does to raise good stock, so you may as well do the job right.

Blue Shubunkins

6. How to Raise Quality Goldfish

Although many people succeed in getting their goldfish to spawn, few successfully rear to maturity even a half-dozen specimens. There are many reasons for their failure. Eggs laid in the fish's natural habitat are in a large amount of shallow water, and the main losses are due to the eggs being eaten by predatory insects, amphibians and other fish (even the parents). The goldfish breeder protects the ova from these predators in the home breeding tank but there is an added problem: because of the higher tank temperature the purity and surface of the water may be affected in a short time.

Imagine an aquarium containing eggs on the point of hatching —about four days after the spawning. If the setup is well arranged, with plenty of space and light for the plants, all may be well for the moment. If, however, too many plants are included, some of the dense patches will contain decaying portions of plant, and the eggs in this area will probably die and be smothered in fungus.

WATER SURFACE

It is the surface of the water, however, that can present the greatest obstacle to those fry that do manage to hatch. Fry must be able to break the surface "skin" of the water and gulp the air that will inflate the air sacs. If decaying matter is present, the fry will be unable to do this. The scummy surface of the water will act as a sheet through which the fry cannot penetrate. (This has often been tested. A few eggs are placed in a small glass cylinder in water. The cylinder top is covered with fine muslin. Other eggs are kept in the same water but outside the cylinder. The eggs in the cylinder may live as long as 10 days but they do not develop swim bladders, and eventually die. Those outside will show the small glistening marks in their transparent bodies which are the beginning of the bladders.)

During the early stages, then, it is important to keep the surface of the water clean. The best way to do this is to draw a piece of newspaper or tissue paper across it so all scum adheres to the paper and can be removed. Or you can break up the surface scum by aerating the water.

The newly-hatched fry do not have proper mouths. Instead, they have suckers that enable them to cling to the glass sides where they hang, tail downward, like exclamation points. Rarely do all the fry hatch on the same day. Often there are two days between the emergence of the first and the last. This can cause difficulties, for two days is a long time at this stage of growth. The fry that hatch first greatly outstrip the others in size and some may eat their brothers during the first two or three weeks. You can prevent this by removing any exceptionally large specimens.

HYDRA

A more serious cause of loss at this early stage is the presence of Hydra. This is a small fresh-water polyp that adheres to the water plants and the sides of the glass, holding its seven or eight thin tentacles outstretched. If any small creature (such as a fish during its first week of life) brushes against the tentacles, explosive cells are set off and many tiny barbs attached to very fine threads penetrate and enmesh its paralyzed body. Some of these threads are sticky while others inject a paralyzing fluid through the barbs. The fry is eventually pulled into an opening where the Hydra's arms and body join. Here it will be quickly digested. Although the Hydra is very small—usually one-half to three-quarters of an inch —and as thin as fine cotton thread, a number of them can eliminate an entire brood of fry.

To get rid of Hydra, remove the fry and the plants and put a tablespoonful of ammonia in the tank. Examine the glass often for any specimens of Hydra. If the fry are growing well they should be far too strong for Hydra after a week or ten days.

Other creatures which may have been concealed on the spawning plants are leeches and planarians. Snails, of course, devour fish eggs and should not be in the tank.

FEEDING FRY

There are several excellent techniques for feeding your goldfish fry. The best, and certainly the most popular way, is to provide natural food consisting of microscopic forms of animal life known as infusorians. It was once thought that they were spontaneously generated in infusions of vegetable matter. This is not true; they must be cultured.

INFUSORIANS

An average hatching of 500 to 1,000 fry will require a large amount of this food for about two weeks (at 75°). Since you will need time to build up a culture of these protozoa, as soon as the eggs are laid you must decide whether you will use this method. If you decide to use infusorians, you will need many one-quart mason jars (or similar jars). Fill them with water in which hay or lettuce has been scalded and add some of the hay or lettuce to each jar. Within three days each jar should be teeming with a microscopic type of protozoan life, known as the *Paramecium* or slipper animalcule (from its shape). If you have a low-powered microscope or hand lens you can make certain that the culture contains enough of the desired creatures. If you place a drop of the fluid on a piece of clear glass and examine it under a lens, you will see a few hundred of these animalcules milling around. If you see only one or two, the culture is useless.

When the fry first hatch, they do not feed because they have no mouths. During this period they depend for their development and nourishment on the remains of the yolk sac on their ventral surface. In two or three days, depending on the temperature, the sac will be completely absorbed and the fry will swim in search of food. As soon as you see this, add the first jar of the culture to the aquarium. Save pieces of hay or lettuce and a little water. Refill the jar immediately with old aquarium water and another piece of lettuce leaf. This will provide the basis for a new culture to develop from what remains on the old hay or in the water left in the jar. The culture should be ready in two days. If you refill jars as they are used, you will always have an available supply. Do not keep the jars in direct sunlight or the temperature of the water may reach over 100° and the *paramecia* will be cooked. To examine the cultures for progress, you can shine a flashlight through the jars at night. The creatures will reflect light much as an airplane caught in the beam of a searchlight. If the culture is thriving, you will see clouds of silvery specks gracefully gliding in all directions.

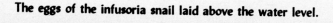

The eggs of the infusoria snail laid above the water level.

Occasionally the infusoria snail (*Ampullaria*) is used to provide food. This is a gigantic creature that produces enormous amounts of microscopic life, due mainly to the large amount of excreta it leaves after devouring lettuce, its favorite food. The infusoria snail, a tropical snail from the Amazon, becomes quite accustomed to indoor cold-water aquariums and breeds prolifically. The egg masses are laid a few inches above the water level on the sides of the aquarium and look like a large mulberry in shape and color. The only trouble with this creature is that it does the job too well and the tank in which it is kept soon begins to smell rather bad.

Modern infusoria pills or powder are now available to take all the work out of infusoria culture.

DAPHNIA

Within two weeks the fish should be ready for a larger diet, usually of sifted *Daphnia*. *Daphnia pulex* is a small fresh-water crustacean found in stagnant pools and still water, sometimes in such quantities that the water appears red. Adult *Daphnia* specimens may range in size from a pin head to a match head. They are far too large for the young fish to ingest. Since *Daphnia* **give birth**

Lionhead goldfish

to young almost continually, you can pour a canful of adult *Daphnia* through fine-meshed wire or coarse muslin. What passes through the screen will contain thousands of larval *Daphnia* (or *nauplii*) which will be ideal for the fry at this stage. You may keep the larger specimens for the adult fish. Feed as much *Daphnia* as fish will eat in one hour.

BRINE SHRIMP

Another very acceptable food is the newly-hatched young of brine shrimp (*Artemia salina*). You can buy brine shrimp eggs dry and hatch them according to the directions.

MOSQUITO RAFTS

For very enthusiastic aquarists there is another method of feeding fry during this period. While you don't have to produce infusoria, this method is probably more troublesome, but it is much more effective for the frys' speed of growth. It involves collecting thousands of mosquito rafts or egg masses. Mosquito rafts will be laid in an exposed tub of manure water or in shallow pans containing water to which dried blood has been added. Carefully collect the rafts as they are laid and place them in mason jars containing fresh water. Store the jars in a warm place. Again timing is important. Some of these rafts must be hatching as the fry are ready to receive their first food.

The emerging larval gnat or mosquito is very small and transparent but it is many times larger than *Paramecia*. You will notice that the fry have trouble eating them at first, but soon they will devour all you provide as they eat these insects continuously. Their growth will be speeded by as much as 100%.

Of course, this is a tedious business. An additional disadvantage is that the mosquito larvae grow faster than the fish. Any not eaten within the first few hours after they hatch will continue to develop. They must be removed before they reach the pupal stage, or they will produce a swarm of mosquitos in the fish room.

ARTIFICIAL FOODS

You may use artificial foods exclusively but the results are seldom satisfactory. The possibility of fouling the water is also much greater. Artificial foods consist of such substances as dried egg or the yolk of hard-boiled egg squeezed through muslin so that it enters the water in the form of a mist. If you use dried egg, watch the bottom of the aquarium for any signs of a bright red color. This indicates a patch where the uneaten powder has fallen. If it is neglected, it will cause conditions that will kill the fry. Any uneaten non-living food will foul the water but fry, as a rule, are much more able to stand slight foulness than adults. In nature, goldfish fry are found in shallows among reeds and in isolated pockets where the water contains much rotting vegetation (the source of their initial food). Dried egg, however, rapidly produces bad conditions if too much is used, so be careful with it. You may introduce snails to the rearing tank to help clean up uneaten food particles, but wait until the fry are free-swimming.

During the first two weeks, watch carefully for any signs of flukes (see page 100). On a badly infected fish the flukes look like a small white beard. If fry continually remain right on the surface of the water, the probable cause is gill fluke that makes breathing difficult. Destroy any fish that are infected with this parasite at this early stage. Carefully remove the rest of the fry to another tank containing clean, aged water of the same temperature and make extra efforts to feed them as heavily as possible with live food.

CULLING

It is sometimes possible to start selecting good specimens during the first two weeks of their life. With the fancy types of goldfish, it is imperative to repeat this selection, or culling, at weekly intervals. A good culling method is to place the entire brood in a white bowl (so that divided finnage may be observed more closely). It is not enough merely to lift out likely youngsters

115

Fantail goldfish.

as they are noticed. Some regular systematic culling method is necessary. Although it may take some hours to go through a whole brood, the results should more than make up for the effort.

First of all you must realize that only the best fish are to be retained. This may seem rather ruthless, but since goldfish are such prolific breeders and the percentage of really good young is so small, it is the only way to build up a decent strain. If you keep too many fry, none will receive proper care and room and the whole collection, including the few good specimens, will become undersized worthless runts.

Before you begin culling, prepare a clean aquarium for the chosen few. If you have only a few tanks, the first culling (when the fish are 14 days old) should yield no more than 100 fish. Dip a white china soup plate into the fry tank and trap 30 or 40 youngsters. Lift the plate out and, with a teaspoon, place those fish that show good divided finnage in a new tank. Do not be surprised if the number of good fish you find seems rather small— four or five out of 40. Fancy goldfish do not breed very true. (Five per cent of good veiltails from even first-class line-bred stock would be an exceptional figure.)

Oranda veiltail

After you have 100 youngsters in a 24 x 12 x 15 aquarium, you can begin to examine them for profile. Destroy any that show irregular or deformed dorsals, turned up snouts, only one eye, and such faults. This will probably reduce the original 100 to about 60. By the end of the first month they should be three-quarters of an inch in length, and they will require spacing out if no further culling is planned. When they reach this size you should not keep more than two dozen in a tank of the size mentioned. Otherwise they will not develop properly. Reduce the number every two weeks, until, at three months, there are no more than eight to a tank.

As the fish increase in size, try to eliminate any that show a single anal fin or an excessively slim body (all the rotund species should have a rotund form). Finally, you should be left with about two dozen specimens with good body shape and finnage. At this stage, for all but those types that have no dorsal fin (lionheads, celestials, etc.), other characteristics will begin to appear. If the fish are of the protruding-eye types, the eye development should begin to appear at 12 weeks, with the whole process completed in another 12 weeks. During this period you may observe some fish with odd eyes—only one protruding or, in the case of celestials, one eye turning upward and one sidewards. These must also be removed. With the fancier types, you will probably end with about a dozen specimens and, if you are lucky, two or three of these might stand a chance in a show. Now you can understand why quality goldfish are worth a great deal of money—so much hard work goes into their production.

SCALE GROUPS

So far the various scale groups found in each type have not been mentioned. This will depend on whether you are breeding for metallic or nacreous specimens. If the fish are metallics, all the young should be the same since the parents are metallic. They are all bronze when young, and if they are to color in the first year you must give them extra heat (80° F.). Many will begin to color

A pair of nacreous calico veiltail goldfish.

at four months; discard as breeders any that do not color within 12 months.

The young of nacreous goldfish will be of the three scale groups. Since each group needs different treatment for best development, you will have to separate them. The metallics are usually the most robust and will require more heat if they are to color. The nacreous types should be reared in opaque water (fairly green water with plenty of surface plants to shield them from strong light). Good colored matts should also be raised in green water because they are the weakest and will fail to develop properly in competition with their stronger brothers. Various methods of producing the beautiful peacock blue color of good Shubunkins have been tried. However, the only method that seems to work is continued selective breeding of the best specimens. Crossing a pink matt fish with a bronze-scaled specimen sometimes produces a few good blues; more often many drab specimens of a slatish color are hatched. *There is no short cut to the production of show fish,* and it is probably just as well, since without the difficulty much of the interest would vanish.

LIONHEADS AND ORANDAS

The best method of breeding the lionhead and Oranda is first to breed from parents that show a well-developed hood and then to select young that have the required body shape and finnage. The lionheads require particular care since their backs, lacking the dorsal fin, often have bumps or dents along the spine which spoil what might otherwise be a perfect specimen. They need patient care for the next 12 months when they should begin to show reasonable development of the hood. Full hood development will not be reached for some years.

Celestial goldfish.

This close-up of a mature male lionhead clearly shows the nature and texture of the hood. Sometimes if the hood is too fully developed it impairs the gills and nostrils of the goldfish.

PEARL-SCALED FANTAILS AND BUBBLE-EYES

Pearl-scaled fantails exhibit their peculiar characteristics at a very early age, so that this type presents no special difficulty in selection. The bubble-eye develops much as the Moor and telescope-eyed types, with the eyes beginning to develop marked bladders beneath them at about the twelfth week. These fish also require careful inspection of their backs, for, like the lionheads, they tend to show an irregular surface.

Above: A close-up of a female bubble-eye goldfish. Her sacs have just collapsed. Below: A young pearl scale goldfish just beginning to show scale formation.

This is a prize-winning pearl scale belonging to Mr. Horeman.

Note the large eyes on this Moor goldfish.

MOORS

Young Moors will look like normal-eyed bronze fantails or veils according to the type. The black color develops along with the gradual protrusion of the eye. If young Moors still appear very bronzy after the full development of the eye, it is unlikely that they will ever become good specimens. They will probably turn red or orange. Many Moors eventually change color and it is exceedingly difficult to produce a strain that will retain a velvet blackness throughout their lives. It is not advisable to keep Moors too warm, either when they are young or when they are adults, for this is one of the many causes of color change.

A pair of celestials in the chase prior to spawning. The male (left) and female seem to keep swimming in tight circles.

CELESTIALS

The celestial has rarely been bred successfully in Europe or America. The eye development is certainly unique. This eye change is fascinating to watch. Although you know that it has a genetic cause, it still seems strange that the eyes, quite normal at birth, should not only begin to protrude but should also gradually turn upward until one eye nearly looks at the other across the top of the head. These fish can see well enough, however, to be trained quickly to accept food from the hand. When you are selecting the young of this type, again notice body shape and finnage for

125

the first 10 or 12 weeks. Then keep a careful watch on the eye development. In some the eyes may remain telescopic; others may develop one celestial eye and one normal protruding eye. A difference in the size of the eyes can completely mar the fish so that there will probably be fewer good specimens of this type than of any other.

A 3-week-old celestial goldfish showing a normal eye.

At 7 weeks of age the eyes begin to turn upward. This is an amazing process, and no one knows why it happens.

This is the same fish illustrated on the opposite page. Here it is 11 weeks old.

Below: The same fish at 6 months, with eyes turned upward. This picture was taken from the top, looking onto the back of the fish.

Oranda goldfish

VEILTAILS

The veiltail, which most people agree is the queen of all gold-fish, requires special care in the selection of the young if the adults are not to become a mass of bedraggled fins. Even with good specimens this will occur with age, for the fins continue to grow, although very slowly, throughout the veil's life. The young that you select should be as rotund as possible. The dorsal fin should be strongly rayed and always held erect. It should show signs of reaching the required final dimensions—equal in height to the body depth. Since quite a number of fantails are produced in any spawning of veils, you should differentiate between them. The best way to do this is to select those specimens that exhibit the longest anals, a sure indication that the tails will eventually follow suit.

Lionhead goldfish,

Oranda goldfish

A female Bristol Shubunkin goldfish.

BRISTOL SHUBUNKINS

Of the single-tailed varieties, the most difficult to produce are Bristol Shubunkins. Really good specimens are rare. The chief fault here is a drooping caudal caused by attempting a standard that is almost impossible. The fish's body must be streamlined, while the caudal fin is expected to be widely spread with very rounded lobes. But with those youngsters that remain streamlined and also have good caudal development, the extended tail starts to droop and if it becomes very wide the body will deepen to support the monstrous tail. Even in the best specimens the caudal peduncle is shortened, although occasionally fish with a really remarkable profile do appear.

The Bristol Shubunkin exhibits the finest coloration of any of the nacreous groups but because of the need for correct finnage it is a difficult type to select when young. The best advice is to select the young that have the deepest color and well-rounded moderate caudals. Any that exhibit large caudals at this time will almost certainly be disappointing.

7. Goldfish Diseases

Fish, like humans, are heir to many diseases. Most diseases come from the same source—*poor living conditions.* You should know about the common illnesses and the parasites. Most diseases are easily prevented or cured. It is important, however, that you recognize the early symptoms of disease, since most diseases are progressive and are more difficult to cure in the later stages. You should also find out the reason for any disease that develops. Disease will usually be your fault: the result of fouling the water with too much food; chill caused by not watching temperatures when changing water; overcrowding; or indigestion from the use of wrong foods. Since speed is all-important in the cure, you should have a small medicine cabinet with the required chemicals and apparatus always on hand.

INDIGESTION

Any fish that behaves in a listless or unbalanced manner should be suspected of illness. Indigestion is the most likely cause if excreta hangs from the vent for any length of time, especially if there are gas bubbles which sometimes cause it to float upright alongside the body of the fish. Do not feed the fish for several days; then feed it with only live food such as *Daphnia,* worms or *Chironomus* larvae. If you treat indigestion promptly, it is not at all serious, but any neglect can be fatal since it may lead to a condition of permanent imbalance where the fish is unable to remain on an even keel and frequently floats upside-down.

FUNGUS

If there are signs of white fungus (*Saprolegnia ferox*), which looks like patches of white cotton on the fins or body, transfer the

131

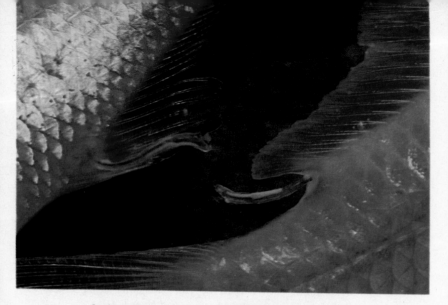

Anchor worms on the skin of goldfish. Photo by Frickhinger.

fish to a salt solution in a small bowl. (Single-tailed fish will jump out if the bowl is not covered.) The solution should be about the strength of sea water: three tablespoons of aquarium salt to the gallon of aquarium water. Sea salt is preferable if you can obtain it; otherwise you may use kosher salt or regular aquarium salt. Do not use the fine, non-clogging salt sold for table use because it contains other ingredients that prevent the normal uptake of moisture.

Keep the fish in the bowl and renew the solution every day until all signs of fungus have gone. This will take from a few days to two weeks depending upon its extent. You may also swab the infected area with a 5% solution of methylene blue, repeating the treatment three times every 24 hours. Before returning the fish to its tank, try to find out why it contracted the fungus. Fungus is caused by loss of natural resistance, since the spores of *Saprolegnia ferox* exist in all water that is exposed to the air. They do not affect a healthy fish, but can only enter a fish that has suffered some physical damage. A fish in normal health is covered with a mucous secreted by the surface cells which are alive. This is why you should not handle a goldfish unless your hands are quite wet and you don't apply any pressure. Fungus infection is the most common of complaints but it is caused by something that has weakened or damaged the fish.

LEECHES AND LICE

Sometimes newly-purchased plants contain such undesirable creatures as leeches or fish lice. You will probably see the leeches. They usually drop off when the plant is sterilized (although this treatment does not kill them). The fish louse, a small free-swimming crustacean of about an eighth of an inch in diameter, is more difficult to see and it sometimes gets into the aquarium. It attaches itself to the body or fins of a fish by means of a spine and it is very difficult to dislodge. You may be able to remove it with tweezers after touching it with a drop of turpentine or iodine. If you find fish lice, watch the fish for any signs of fungus.

ICH

Ich (*Ichthyophthirius*) or white spot is a parasite complaint caused by the protozoan *Ichthyophthirius multifiliis,* which penetrates the surface skin of the fish and feeds on its tissue. The characteristic white spot is the cyst that develops. Although Ich is usually more troublesome with tropical fish, it does occur with cold-water fish and can be difficult to eradicate.

This parasite reproduces by division. The cyst formed by the union of two individuals finally ruptures to shed hundreds of small parasites from the fish into the water. The speed of this dropping-off process varies with temperature, so it is advisable to raise the temperature immediately into the eighties, no matter what method of treatment you use.

Various patent remedies containing quinine are available. They are the most valuable means of controlling Ich. Methylene blue has also been used. Most aquarists recommend the use of a very weak solution: two to three drops of a 5% solution per gallon, but goldfish can stand more of this chemical. Even young fish of little more than one inch in length can tolerate a solution so strong that the blue color completely obscures them when they are not close against the glass or on the surface, so overdose rather than underdose if you are guessing about the dosage. But a strong solution will kill all plants if they remain in it too long, so watch your plants as well as the fish, and change the water if necessary. The fish should be in this solution for approximately two weeks (on and off) for a complete cure.

Another method of curing Ich involves only the use of salt. Here the salt is not dissolved as it is for fungus, but it is added in the proportion of a quarter of a pound to the gallon of water, so that it lies undisturbed on the bottom. After a day or two you will notice that the lower half-inch or inch has formed a layer of denser fluid that has an oily movement as the fish disturb it. This takes a long time to diffuse through the tank. You should change all the salt and water every four days. Even after the change, there will be two layers. Do not use the mixture for very weak fish. They will not have the strength to keep above the strong solution and will probably lie in it. For weak fish, make up a weak solution (one ounce to the gallon) and change it morning and night until the fish recovers. This gradually washes away any free-swimming parasites and the fish will soon benefit from the treatment.

POND PEST

The symptoms of Pond Pest or Red Pest (*Bacterium cyprinicida*) are blood-red patches appearing on the fish's body. It is chiefly caused by foul conditions in the aquarium. Another cause is the use of improperly cleansed live foods such as *Tubifex rivulorum*. Keep the fish in a salt solution of one ounce to the gallon until it is cured. Renew the solution every day. Clean the aquarium thoroughly and wash all plants, stones and gravel.

DROPSY

A fish that is bloated, with scales that start to lift at the free edge, has dropsy. This is an incurable complaint that often comes

The photographer chopped a hole in the ice and took a picture of these veiltails. The fish on the bottom has dropsy. Note the extended scales.

after long periods at a low temperature. Zinc-free malachite has supposedly brought about cures, but the fish will again show the symptoms at the slightest chill. Although a fish with dropsy may live many months, it is best to destroy it immediately.

ANCHOR WORM

Sometimes a fish may have small pimples or boils that have a small thread protruding from the center. The thread, if touched, disappears. The cause is anchor worm (*Lernoea*). Carefully dab each swelling with turpentine, taking care that it touches only the affected area. You can also use ammonia, but it is not as safe.

GAS

If fish are exposed to too much sunshine, especially if the aquarium water is new, gases may enter the circulatory system. The fins, especially the caudal, then become spotted with large bubbles which cause the fish to float head downwards. You can cure this gaseous embolism only by completely changing the water and shielding the aquarium from the light to check the rapid growth of free algae. You must attend to this condition at once, or there will be great damage to the fins, with other illness following.

CONGESTED VEINS

The long-tailed varieties of goldfish sometimes show a reddening around the free margin of the caudals. This symptom may spread to the other fins in advanced stages. In the early stages, especially in red-colored fish, this is not particularly noticeable. But gradually the area becomes blood-red and the congested veins which cause the color break down and the fins become torn and ragged. A parasite (*Cyclochaeta*) has been found connected with this complaint in its advanced stages, but it is very doubtful that it is the initial cause. It is more likely the result of a general lowering of the fish's vitality (as in the case of fungus). Long periods of low temperature when fish are outdoors in the winter, heavy feeding just before a fall in temperature, insufficient live or green food—any of these factors can produce this condition. If the fins are torn and bleeding you may have to trim them with a sharp scissors.

TAIL ROT

A neglected fish may develop tail rot, the breaking up of the caudal fin. In such a case you must remove all affected finnage. If the rot enters the caudal peduncle it is unlikely that the fish will recover. After you remove the damaged portion, paint the stump with 5% methylene blue and keep the fish in a weak solution of salt (one ounce to the gallon). An even better remedy for this

Comet goldfish.

slime bacterial condition is 250 milligrams of tetracycline per gallon of water, each day for a week. The infected fish should be treated in a small hospital tank and remain in the solution all day.

If you think cold is the cause of tail rot, slowly raise the temperature of the water to 60° F.

Sometimes this condition will appear during quite warm weather. The cause then is improper feeding. Plenty of live food and Duckweed will cure it, although it may be necessary to revert to the salt bath. After a fish's tail has been completely removed, it will take a long time for a new tail to grow to normal length again —possibly a year or more. If the fish remains otherwise healthy there is little to worry about. It will be able to swim just as fast (possibly faster if it is of the long-tailed Shubunkin type), although it may be inclined to wobble a little. Fin replacement is usually rapid if the damage is confined to the free edges and affects only the finer rays. It is only when the main rays are severed or damaged that complete recovery takes a long time.

ULCERATION

Ulceration of the fish, accompanied by a filminess of the eyes and swollen gills, is caused by a fungoid disease known as *Achlya*. It must be treated swiftly, with the same method as that used for fungus (page 131). Ulceration, like other diseases, will not occur unless environmental conditions are bad. In addition to treating the fish, you must thoroughly clean and sterilize the aquarium (you can use a pink solution of potassium permanganate).

METAL POISON

Goldfish may become ill and die when no apparent disease is present, although fungus usually appears before death. Metal poisoning may be the cause. Metal poisoning may come from sheet zinc used as an aquarium cover. If the inside of your tank or cover has been left unpainted, as the zinc oxidizes the resulting dust falls into the aquarium at the slightest knock or vibration. Zinc is particularly poisonous to fish, as are other common metals and alloys such as brass, copper and bronze. Be sure that there is no corrosive metal in contact with the water or in such a position that corrosion can affect the water.

SPAWNING INJURIES

Female fish that have been injured during spawning (this should not occur in an aquarium unless rocks have been left in) are best treated in an isolation tank where they can be fed on live foods. Watch the wounded areas carefully for any sign of disease. Usually such fish recover completely in a matter of days. Even if all the ventral scales have been lost, they are replaced within a month. But living conditions must be good since the damage is an open door to disease.

A female metallic veiltail showing severe damage to her ventral scales. They were injured during spawning in a new concrete pond. The fish fully recovered.

CHEMICALS

Many chemicals have been recommended as cures for various diseases. However, we have found that most of them are too poisonous for successful use, and more fish die from the treatment than from the actual disease.

Mercurochrome and quinine sulphate are often used. They may very well be effective, but continued use eventually weakens the fish. This will not happen if you use salt or methylene blue. The tolerance of fish for chemicals varies enormously so that *all cases must be treated individually.* Keep the fish in a chemical solution under constant observation. Even when you use the salt treatment, watch the initial reaction of the fish. If the fish has a tendency to keel over, a weaker solution is required. It is usually better to give the ailing fish a quick bath in a strong solution than a protracted bath in a weak solution. This applies especially to potassium permanganate. A strong solution, however, has a harmful effect upon the gill membrane and may in some cases produce a condition that results in the death of the fish.

AN OUNCE OF PREVENTION

With proper attention most diseases can be prevented. Remember that prevention is always better than cure. Never add any plants or fish to the aquarium until they have been in quarantine. After the plants are sterilized, change the water each day for two or three days. During this time keep the plants where they have sufficient light and room (an old mason jar is ideal).

Quarantine the fish for at least a week. Then, if they seem healthy, introduce them to the aquarium. If any fish shows signs of uneasiness or illness, even slight, move it to a separate bowl for a few days, for observation and a mild salt bath. Examine the aquarium for bad conditions (snails have a habit of dying in odd corners behind plants where their putrefying remains can soon cause trouble). Remove uneaten food, fish excreta and mulm or detritus regularly. Also remove any plant leaves that are becoming yellow. This takes only a few minutes daily and saves hours of trouble later. Maintaining healthy fish is merely a matter of applying common sense once you understand the initial requirements.

8. The Garden Pool

Everyone who has successfully kept goldfish in an aquarium and who also has a garden eventually makes a goldfish pool. This requires a different approach from indoors because of exposure to the weather. But a garden goldfish pool is a fascinating project.

The first point to consider is the general design and layout: will the pool be formal or informal, will it be built up or situated in a sunken garden? If the construction is being done for you, you can choose the style that appeals to you most. If, however, you are to be both designer and builder, you should spend a little time thinking about such points as building a wooden mold (shuttering) to hold the wet concrete in position, the amount of soil to be shifted and what to do with it. Also consider the amount of free time at your disposal—some of the best designs need a great deal of work.

The welfare of the fish naturally affects all designs. Of great importance is the finished depth of the pool. Since this depth should be at least 3 feet, a sunken garden will obviously require the removal of a considerable amount of soil. If this is too troublesome, or if your space is too limited, you can make a pool within a rockery. What is excavated will form the basis of the rockery, and you won't have to remove so much soil to gain the required depth.

The formal pool is much simpler to build than the informal. You can easily fix and strut the necessary shuttering and achieve a neat, symmetrical finish. Moreover, it is easy to render with sand and cement to obtain a watertight job and when you trowel afterward you can quickly have a perfectly smooth finish. But the result, however neatly executed, can never rival the informal pool for beauty and attraction.

The informal pool is much more difficult to make. If you plan

Pearl scale goldfish

to build one, first model it in some soft material such as modeling clay. Otherwise the result may disappoint you. The informal pool should appear natural when finished. You must provide properly for the various marginal and marsh or bog plants that will give the final finish. To do this you will need shelving in the concrete surface, with the last shelf for the bog almost at water level. There should also be a shallow depression in the area required for the plants. This should be filled with suitable soil that will remain saturated.

If it is possible, it is a good idea to have two ponds, one at a higher level than the other so that a waterfall joining the two can flow. (Water will have to be pumped from the lower pool to the upper, for return via the fall.) It will provide the music of running water and will also attract the birds for a daily bath in the troughs of the fall. You will be able to spend many pleasant hours there, and its great beauty and interest will make the difficulty of construction worth while.

DEEP SPOTS

Remember that the pool is primarily for the fish. It should have at least one spot deep enough to prevent discomfort in very hot weather and to provide security in very cold. (Fish suffer more hardship in unheated aquaria located in unheated glass houses than they do at the bottom of frozen ponds. This is because the water in aquaria can and does reach 32° F. though it remains ice-free, but the water at the bottom of a pond, even though a foot of ice covers it, is usually no colder than 39° F., the temperature at which water has the greatest density.)

During very harsh weather fish like to burrow right into the mud. Although clay can discolor water if it is disturbed by feeding fish, some clay at the deepest spot is better than an accumulation of rotting detritus (which will probably drift over the top of gravel or sand). But in a small pond keep clay or soil to a minimum.

SHALLOWS

In addition to a deep spot, the pond should have a shallow area where the fish may spawn properly. This area should be big enough so that you may observe the fish freely. Fish will spawn in water of any depth, but in deeper water they usually lay their eggs on or near the surface. Since plant fronds are sparse in such a depth, most of the eggs will be lost in the mud or will become attached to water lily stems where they will be immediately devoured. Before the fish lay their eggs it seems necessary for them to obtain a hold on plants or some firm object. If there are no shallows, the fish will probably use the perimeter of the pond and damage their fins and scales as they thresh about against the concrete side. Eggs deposited in this region are usually lost because it is almost impossible to remove them without damage, even if they are attached to short algae or blanket weed.

FINISHING THE POOL

Take great care as you finish the pool. Any small projections will tear the sides and fins of the fish if they become lively and start jumping. When completed, fill the pond and allow it to stand for a few days to test for leakage. Then, if all is well, run off or pump out the water, as it contains far too much lime from the cement to be healthy for the fish. (If the pond is on the shallow side, the concentration of lime would be sufficient to cause the fishes' death by breaking down their protective mucous covering and exposing them to disease.) After you empty the pond it is a good plan to sponge it down with ordinary vinegar, wiping any surplus that may drain to the deepest part. Then you can fill and stock the pool with safety.

PLANTS

First put in your aquatic plants and give them time to settle in. The types of plants (especially marginals) suitable for the goldfish pool vary with the pool's design, but usually the larger types are barred because of their vigorous growth. Choose water lilies from the medium and smaller types; the deep-water varieties grow too fast and produce too many big leaves. One of the best varieties is *Marliacea chromatella*. It has many blossoms and handsome, medium-size foliage. It will grow well in 2 to 3 feet of water and produce many cream-colored flowers. If you have room—a pond 12 feet or more in length—you can offset this lily with another free-flowering variety, the N. James Brydon. These blooms are deep pink or red.

For small pools, plant the lilies in large pots filled with good loam with a little aged cow manure at the bottom. Since lily stalks and leaves are heavily vacuolated (have many air pockets to make

This is a close-up of a water lily, photographed after a shower.

This is a magnificent informal pool composed of an upper pond, a series of water steps or falls, and a lower pond. There are many advantages to a setup like this one. The water is continually circulated and aerated and the younger fish can be separated from the breeders. A pump is necessary to bring the water back from the lower pond to the upper.

them buoyant) you will need some method of holding them down. It is not uncommon for the whole root system to be withdrawn from the pot, with the plant floating in an untidy tangled mess. The best way to hold water lilies down is to encrust the lip of the pot with a rim of concrete that overlaps toward the center and adds weight to the pot, since it may be lifted too. Do not place new lily crowns straight into deep water since they may rot without sufficient light. It is best to place them in the shallow portion of the pool until they have made a good start, when they may be moved gradually to their final position. Before planting the crowns, examine them for any undesirable creatures—leeches and such are very difficult to eradicate once they are established.

Springtime is, of course, the best time for planting. Then all the plants will have the best chance to develop before winter sets in, and those that develop roots will become firmly established before they die down. Others, such as Hornwort, Frogbit, and some of the Potomogetons will have a chance to develop the winter buds that will sink to the bottom as winter approaches and rise again in the spring to form new plants.

Plants obtained as cuttings must be firmly anchored to the bottom in clumps by means of lead wire. The plants will greatly vary in their growth, and you should use only a few of the more rampant species—for example, *Elodea canadensis, Elodia crispa, Fontinalis antipyretica,* and the Potomogetons. Many of these are useful as spawning media and food for the fish, and most are good oxygenators, helping to keep the water from turning green. Therefore you should include a few in the pond.

Cabomba caroliniana is a plant that is seldom grown in cold water. But once it is established it will thrive and give a wonderful display, like underwater pine trees. In tropical aquaria the whorls seldom exceed 2 inches in diameter, but in cold water, after the plant has passed several winters under thick ice, the whorls reach an astounding size, some measuring more than 5 inches across. However, some of the rampant types already mentioned will quickly cover it.

For the very shallow parts of the pond the Crowfoot (*Ranun-*

Water Hawthorn, *Aponogeton distachyon*, is an ideal shallows plant.

culus aquatilis) is one of the prettiest plants, but it requires a rich soil to flower well. Other plants suitable for the shallows are the Water Hawthorn (*Aponogeton distachyon*); Water Violet (*Hottonia palustris*); *Ludwigia mullerti*; Bog Bean (*Calla palustris*), and Forget-Me-Not (*Myosotis*). Some of the pigmy varieties of water lily such as *Helvolia* may also find a place here for they will do well in six inches of water. Do not use the large types of the taller bog plants unless you have a large pool. They increase rapidly and make a great deal of root. This group includes *Typha latifolia;* Giant Spearwort (*Ranunculis lingua*); the Flowering Rush (*Butumus umbellatus*); Pickerel Weed (*Pontederia cordata*), and some of the larger irises. More suitable types for the small pool

This picture of an upper pond shows the details of the steps and falls and the way it is planted with water plants and bog plants. A rock garden also adorns the sides.

This formal pool contains only a few fish. There is a large celestial goldfish poking its eyes and head clear out of the water. This pool is primarily designed for breeding and increasing the size of fancy fish.

are *Typha minima,* a dwarf bulrush with a round seed-head and a maximum height of 18 inches; Giant Sagittaria, which will make aerial leaves and finally put up a flower head 12 to 18 inches above the water level; the dwarf irises (*Iris sibirica*), and the Marsh Marigold (*Caltha palustris*).

For bright color at the water's edge, the various types of Mimula are unrivaled for range of color and length of flowering. If you can grow ferns in the crevices between rocks, especially where there is a waterfall, you will greatly enhance the general appearance of the pool. It takes time for these plants to develop properly.

CLEANING THE POOL

Remove all dead and dying portions of plants from a pool during the autumn or any gases formed by their decomposition will be trapped under ice and will asphyxiate the fish. Carefully watch the formation of ice on a pond. When it is about one inch thick remove a small area (a square foot or less) and take out a few gallons of water so that a warm pocket is formed. You can then temporarily seal the opening with a burlap bag. This bag will also serve as a kind of inspection cover which you may lift occasionally to see if the water is reasonably good. However, if it isn't, because you neglected to remove dead plants and so forth, it will be hard to do anything about it during the cold weather.

Pools naturally become very green in the spring. Running in fresh water will not help—quite the reverse, in fact. If the pool has been properly planted, leave it alone. The trouble will clear as the plants begin to grow and the water lilies will prevent any recurrence by limiting the amount of sunlight entering the water. *Do not* use chemicals to clear the water; *do* be especially careful with the amount of dried food you use while the plants are growing.

Blanket weed (*Cladophera*) will usually make an appearance sooner or later. Since the filaments are strong enough to damage the finnage of some fish you should keep it down as much as possible. If you leave it alone, it will smother everything and be almost impossible to remove without replanting the whole pool. Twirl a stick in the water among the growth to gather it up quickly. Then you can lift it out easily. You must do this regularly, and before the weed has had time to twine among the other plants.

Periodically you should clean the pool well. Remove everything and scrub the inside with a stiff broom. Examine the plants for undesirable creatures before returning them to the pool (it is quite surprising what you may find after two or three years). This kind of thorough cleaning should be necessary only every few years. How often it is needed will depend upon your care of the pool. However careful you are, of course, there will come a time when a spring cleaning is clearly indicated.

GOLDFISH IN THE POOL

If your pool is purely ornamental, with the fish present to add color and movement, choose the common goldfish, Comet and Shubunkin or metallic fantail. If they have enough room, they will be very hardy. Do not cram your pool to capacity. Hot sultry evenings will only cause the fish distress, if not death, and the fish will not develop but will tend to become dwarfed or stunted. It is a good plan to allow no more than one fish to every two square feet of surface area.

Many people imagine that fish in an outside pool do not require feeding. While this may be true in an old established pool containing a few fish, it is not at all true if the pool is a new one. Many fish die in the spring because of this erroneous opinion. Fish hibernate in the winter, living on fat stored during the summer feeding. If the amount of food available did not provide enough fat, the fish will awaken from hibernation half-starved and weak and be exposed to many of the fish diseases. People often say: "Oh, I kept the fish through the winter all right, but they all got fungus and died in the spring." Of course they did if they weren't fed sufficiently in late summer and autumn.

You may feed them all the usual foods (see pages 12-14). If

151

This koi pool is relatively shallow at 20 inches deep. Shallow pools show
the fish off very well, but they must be protected from the hot sun and
prevented from freezing over. Photo courtesy Kodansha.

152

A 4-year-old female Golden Orfe suitable for a large outdoor pool.

you use dried foods, such as chopped shrimp or biscuit, watch the fish and be sure that they eat all that you give. In this way you will not foul the bottom of the pool—an important point when ice covers the surface. In the spring, remove any fish that show signs of sickness, give them a salt bath and feed them on garden worms. They should make a speedy recovery.

Occasionally fish will change color. In metallics, this is usually due to the reappearance or disappearance of black pigment; in nacreous fish other colors may also come and go. The color change does not necessarily mean any change in health, although black pigment will probably appear at a spot where some injury has been sustained.

Watch the movement of fish in the pool so you can immediately spot any that behave in a strange manner. Lift them out and examine them more closely for leeches or fish lice. A fish that is inclined to wobble may be consumptive. This disease generally appears with age, and there is no cure.

Fancy goldfish, with the exception of the Comet, Shubunkin and metallic fantails, are not usually considered very hardy. Even though this is far from true, the fish are valuable (many are worth $50 to $100 apiece) and they have excessive finnage and other peculiarities, so keep them where you can easily observe their condition.

It is wrong for the pool temperature to be 60° F. and above. Such warmth weakens the fish and hinders breeding. Spawning seems to be initiated when goldfish awaken from a period of hibernation.

Fancy goldfish that have been kept in open pools at various times have seemed the better for it. Fish from a coddled strain do develop dropsy or swim bladder trouble, but in successful breeding this is part of building up a virile and hardy strain.

You may have to keep an open pool covered (perhaps with wire mesh) when you are away, to protect the fish from cats and birds. Rats and snakes may also remove small goldfish and certain types of frogs will devour them. If you keep small fish (of 3 to 6 months) in a pond, be certain that the larval form of the larger

Above: Dragonfly larvae are dangerous, because they can kill goldfish fry. Remove them whenever you see them. Below: *Dytiscus* beetle larva. The powerful pincers can make short work of small fish.

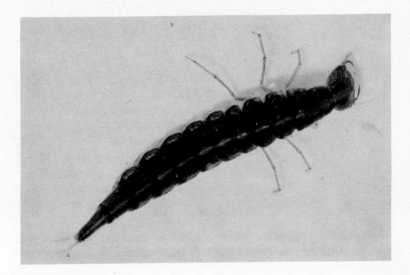

This pond extends under the house and contains some 200 koi ranging in length from 16 to 32 inches. Photo courtesy Kodansha.

This pool is covered at one end to keep the algae from blooming and turning the water green. Photo courtesy Kodansha.

types of dragonflies is absent as well as the larvae of such water beetles as *Hydrophilus piceus* and *Dytiscus marginalis*. They are quite capable of killing fish smaller than 2 inches in length.

Many dealers recommend including water terrapin in pools. Avoid terrapins larger than 2 inches in diameter, as they are quite skillful at capturing even the fast-moving minnow and they have large appetites.

BREEDING

If you keep more than one type of goldfish in the pool and wish to breed them, watch for signs of spawning. Then move the desired fish to an aquarium or handspawn them and return them to the pool. Any eggs in the pool will probably be of mongrel strain. Leave them for the fish to devour.

Goldfish, if left entirely alone in a pool, will breed and produce a few young if there are good solid banks of underwater plants. The number of young, however, will be small and there is no guarantee that the best will survive. The reverse is more likely, and in a summer with not enough or too much sun the youngsters probably will not grow enough to enable them to last through the winter. If you do want a few young fish, then remove some of the ova and rear the young at a reasonable temperature (70 to 75° F.) for at least the first three months of their lives. You can safely transfer them to the pool in late July or early August (when the water should be around 70° F.). They will still have time to develop a good deal before winter sets in, by which time they should be at least 2 to 2½ inches long.

It is not a good plan to include other varieties of cold-water fish with fancy goldfish. The single-tailed goldfish varieties, however, will hold their own with some other fish. Among them are the Golden Tench, a handsome yellow fish of quiet habits that is inclined to grow large (specimens weighing 2 pounds are not uncommon); the Golden Rudd, a handsome fish that lives on the surface; the Golden Orfe, and the Japanese Golden Carp. The carp grows to an immense size—10 or 12 pounds—in a very short time, but it is a docile and harmless fish. The Golden Orfe also grows quickly to 12 or 18 inches in length, but it is not as docile. It will devour small goldfish or bite the caudal fin completely off, usually causing the death of the fish since part of the caudal peduncle is also removed. The Orfe requires a higher oxygen content than goldfish or carp and will be in trouble during sultry weather if the pool is shallow or small. It is a beautiful fish, however, and a pool is more attractive for having it.

FEEDING TIME

Train your fish to come to a given spot in the pool to receive their food. Use some sort of signal to indicate that it is feeding time. You can slap one of the surrounding stones with the flat of

A well-managed pool is one in which the goldfish will assemble at a particular corner to be fed. Goldfish are definitely creatures of habit.

Natural rocks add to the beauty of koi ponds and can also be used to make paths through the gardens around the ponds. This pond supports 40 to 50 koi ranging in size from 12 to 24 inches. Photo courtesy Kodansha.

your hand before each feeding, or you can use a bell or whistle. Training is not difficult, for fish learn quickly. After two or three weeks they should all be dashing to the spot at the signal. Thus you will always be able to show visitors the special fish that you are proud of. Nothing is more disappointing than to show your friends a beautiful pool that seems completely empty because your approaching footsteps made the fish disappear from view.

160

9. Koi, Japanese Imperial Colored Carp

Do you know any fish which changes color as it gets older? Perhaps you don't, for there are very few freshwater fishes which completely change color as they mature (but many coral fishes go through complete color changes as they grow). About the only freshwater fish that I can bring to mind that dramatically changes color is the Japanese Imperial Colored Carp, called **Koi** or **Goi**. Both words, *Koi* and *Goi* mean *carp* in the Japanese language and the same Japanese character can be read in either accent.

Taisho-Sanke

But why should an article about koi appear in a Goldfish book? Because these colored carp are the most expensive and colorful of all pool fishes; because we've just learned that they are the most efficient scavengers for the pool and aquarium; because we've just learned that more koi are sold every year than any other single fish including the goldfish; because we've just learned that koi grow to fit the size of the container in which they are kept (they can be dwarfed for a small aquarium or can reach 30 inches in a large pool); because imports of koi have reached major proportions and they are now being sold in many of the aquarium shops all over the world. I doubt that there is an aquarium shop in Los Angeles, Tokyo, Honolulu or London that can't supply you with koi.

The Asagi, or light blue, koi which is fairly common.

If you were ever to study music seriously, you would find that most of the notations and remarks dealing with music have their basis in the Italian language. If you wish to study koi, you will have to be satisfied with using the Japanese language, since all of the different koi varieties are described with Japanese words that have been ac-

The Kanoho, a very rare color variety in which the scales are edged in gold.

A beautiful Ohgon koi with almost metallic scales.

The Taisho-Sanke, or three-colored Koi from the Taisho era, 1911-1924.

A moss rock-tile pond at the East-West Center of the University of Hawaii.

Tile koi pond owned by Stanley G. Maeshiro of Hawaii.

Both koi with large scales combined with naked areas and koi that are completely scaleless are generally referred to as Doitsu. This includes the mirror carp (shown here) and the leather carp (scaleless form). Photo by Ken Lucas, Steinhart Aquarium.

The Ki-Bekko has yellow as the main color with accents of black. Photo courtesy Kodansha.

A mixed
population of koi
showing good
specimens of
many color
varieties.

The Asagi is a koi variety that usually has a net-like pattern around the scales. The back is blue or gray, while the cheeks, fins, and lower parts are at least partial red or orange. Photo courtesy Kodansha.

cepted in the koi trade. While most koi are still bred in Japan, many are raised in England, Italy and the United States. I believe I brought the first koi into the United States and bred them in Florida in 1969. This was the first time koi were bred in a warm climate. When it came time to sell them, I used the Japanese names for the fish (see page 209), and most of these names are still used to this day.

In order to learn about breeding koi, I went to Japan and visited many koi farms. This was in 1968. I was amazed at the thousands of acres of scarce Japanese farmland being devoted to

Holding and rearing ponds for koi such as those shown here are a fairly common sight in many Japanese towns.

Beautifully colorful water lilies heighten the attractiveness of any koi pool in which they are used.

This is a Shiro-Bekko Ginrin. Shiro-Bekko koi have the main color white with accents of black, while the Ginrin refers to the glistening silvery scales on the fish's back. Photo courtesy Kodansha.

Mrs. Axelrod hand-feeding koi. The koi is an Ohgon type.

Shown in the foreground is one of the many lakes that lie at the foot of Mount Fujiyama in Japan; Mt. Fuji itself is in the background. The pen-like structure in the lake is used for fish culture.

the breeding and rearing of koi, but I soon learned that these fish bring up to $50,000 each if they are prize winners—and that the ones that don't do well at all are eaten.

At each farm I visited, I was treated as an honorary fish farmer and guest, so I was invited to participate in one of their delightful customs. After each visit, I would be shown a very beautiful large koi, say about 18 inches long. It would always be a very valuable, colorful fish. The fish would be netted and ceremoniously killed by having the head cut off! The fish would then be skinned, boned and served with a soy sauce, to be eaten raw and almost still wriggling. I

The winner of the All Japan Koi Show with his trophy.

第一回 全日本総合錦鯉品評会

These are the trophies that were awarded to winners in the different classes at the first All-Japan koi show held in late 1968.

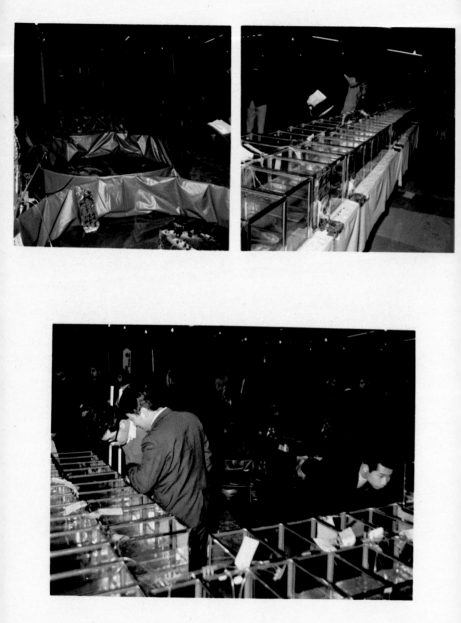

Various views of the show floor at the first All-Japan koi show.

was later told that fresh koi are really very much like the fresh carp that are still to this day sold alive in eastern Europe for holidays. The fish are usually taken home and smoked or cooked, but they are sold alive in every fish market in Poland during the season. In Japan a meal of fresh, raw koi costs about $75 per person (without melon or coffee . . . that costs an extra $18!!).

This is a Japanese
moss rock type
Koi garden.

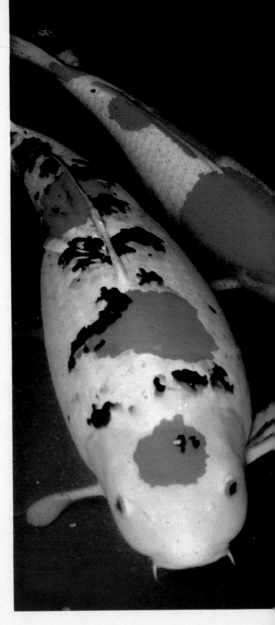

This Taisho
Sanke was one of
the major award
winners at the
first All-Japan
koi show held in
Tokyo in 1968.

181

A Kohaku (or Gin Goke). Gin-Goke means silver scale. This was the first color variety of colored carp.

The Shiro-Utsuri, which is mostly black on white.

Aka-muji koi.

The accompanying photographs show the various fish farms I visited, scenes of the shows and elaborate trophies, and some of the beautiful gardens. Not much more can be said about the care and feeding of koi than has already been said about the goldfish, since both are very closely related both biologically and as far as their care and feeding are concerned. While goldfish do better with occasional feedings of live foods, koi have a longer intestine and don't require any live foods. Koi really are colored carp, and they do very well as scavengers if enough food is left on the bottom to feed them. While they can live in lakes, they also thrive in slowly running water, but they cannot live in fast-moving streams or rivers.

The triangular red marking on the head of this basically all-white koi shows it to be a Tancho variety of Kohaku koi.

This Kohaku koi would be considered to be a good specimen if it weren't for the red spot below its eye on the cheek area.

Koi holding ponds situated in a mountain lake.

These holding crates are used for separating various types of koi.

Left, a fish culturist netting young koi from a rearing pond. Right, a Japanese koi auction. Prospective buyers have a chance to inspect the koi at close range.

Both koi are Kohaku.

At center of photo,
Kin-ki-utsuri koi.

At center, Asagi.

At center, Ohgon koi.

Koi are truly fish pets and they readily become tame and feed from anyone's hand. Many koi farms sell food and allow guests to roam the farm feeding the fish.

If you are lucky enough to have a house with a garden, why not consider a Japanese garden with a koi pond? It need be only a bit larger than a goldfish pond; even most goldfish ponds will do—but the more space that is made available to koi, the better they will do.

Most of the aquarium stores that normally sell goldfish also sell koi. Usually they have them in the spring, when most people get their goldfish ponds back into condition. If your aquarium store doesn't have the koi you want, in the size and price range you want order them.

In Japan the source of fresh running water is from the melting snows.

The koi are spawned in small pools and the eggs are transferred to large, dirt-bottom ponds to grow up.

Hundreds of thousands of koi-lovers visit the koi shows held throughout Japan.

Koi are shipped around the world in large plastic bags filled 75% with oxygen and 25% with water.

The prizes on display at the All Japan 1968 Koi Show in Tokyo.

A koi auction during which koi wholesalers and dealers bid for koi without knowing what they will get.

Koi rearing ponds are always in valleys between mountains so the running water from the mountains can irrigate the pools.

Judges inspect the koi not only for color, but for health, condition and weight.

This is a Japanese Koi garden. It is certainly within the means of every middle-class Japanese family to own their own Koi garden. A koi pool like this one, excluding the cost of the fish, costs about two weeks wages.

In the fall, when the leaves begin to turn color, the koi are also supposed to change color and the pools are drained.

Koi dealers separate the koi into holding vats where they are sorted according to size. This is a self-service business. Customers catch their own fish.

Small koi are usually a drab gray when they are small, and there is no way that anyone can predict with any accuracy what an individual fish will look like. By breeding champion fish together, though, you have a better chance of raising more colorful fish than if you bred fish already rather dull in coloration. The selection of koi when they are colorless youngsters is based upon their physique and how it conforms to the standards of shape and size. Color comes later. It's fun to buy a few dozen colorless fry early in the spring. You can feed them a good goldfish or koi food (don't use trout or catfish "chows," as they are not suitable) and watch them

193

Calternifolius variegatus, the umbrella plant, is a favorite landscape plant among pool owners.

grow and change colors as they get larger. Perhaps you might also buy a few gold metallic Ohgons, or some other oddity, just to be sure that you have some variety in your pond.

Koi cannot, as a rule, be kept in an aquarium unless the aquarium is very large. A few 4-inch-long koi in a 50-gallon aquarium might have a chance to grow to 6 or 8 inches, but the same 4-inch-long koi could reach 18 inches during the same time if

This European mirror carp, a variety of *Cyprinus carpio*, exhibits the large scales characteristic of the Doitsu type of koi. Older specimens of both carp and Doitsu koi often lose the scales along the sides through abrasion with objects in water.

As the ponds become shallow, fish farmers walk into the ponds and begin netting the fish. Koi, like their ancestors, carp, do well in mud-bottom ponds.

At the Yoshida farm some of the ponds are almost a mile long; scores of workers are needed to collect the koi as the water recedes in the pond.

This is the view a prospective bidder gets when he comes to the fish auction. He cannot really see the color or condition of the fish he is buying.

The cattail, genus *Typha*, is a tall pool-side plant that adds interest and beauty to the koi pond.

Koi ponds are not strictly the preserve of people who live in areas having warm year-round climates. This pond, in which the fish are left
outdoors during the winter even though the pond becomes completely
covered with ice, is in New Jersey.

Doitsu Ohgon; this specimen exhibits a good scale pattern along the lateral line, which is much desired in all Doitsu type koi.

Beni-Kujaku koi; note unblemished whiteness of the extended pectoral fin.

Poor specimen of the Ohgon variety.

Shiro-muji koi should be as completely monochromatic as possible.

The asymmetrical pattern of the lateral scalation of this Doitsu Sanke detracts from the value of the fish as a show specimen.

An albino koi showing the pink eyes characteristic of true albinos; albino koi bred to each other will breed true.

Pelleted fish food can be used in your outdoor pool as well as your home aquarium. You will find that most pet shops carry both floating and sinking brands of pool pellets.

Freeze-dried tubifex worms and other meaty freeze-dried foods (such as mosquito larvae, daphnia, zooplankton, and brine shrimp) are excellent growth-stimulating foods for koi.

Aquatic plants play a very important role in the koi pool through their capacity for shading the water from the direct rays of the sun, thereby helping to control the proliferation of algae while regulating the temperature of the water.

Even a close inspection of the fish to be auctioned wouldn't do much for the prospective buyer. He merely bids for a number. They do know who is the breeder of each batch of koi, and the amount bid depends upon the reputation of the breeder. There is a lot of honor involved in all Japanese business dealings.

In the winter the koi are handled exactly like the summer. Because the pools are so deep, they do not freeze.

The three-colored koi at the bottom of the picture, almost out of sight, won the show and was sold for $20,000. This is the final judging where they had the best five koi all together and finally had to select one.

Sometimes the winner of the koi auction only takes a few fish that he needs for breeding and sells the rest right on the spot. He then puts the koi in a plastic bag with oxygen and walks them home, as proud of his new fish as a woman with a bouquet of flowers.

A moss rock-tile outdoor pool housing koi; this pond is at the Pineapple Research Institute of Hawaii.

Closeup of the waterfall area of a moss rock type pond.

The flowering rush, *Butomus umbellatus*, is a hardy plant that does well in koi pools and adds a highly decorative touch.

The center fish is
a representative
of the Asagi
variety.

208

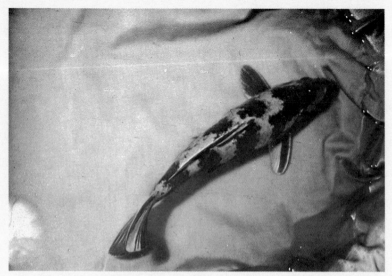

The Kin-ki-utsuri koi is very similar to the Ki-utsuri and Hi-Utsuri varieties but differs in being highly metallic.

The white coloration in the Shiro-utsuri should be evenly dispersed over the body, not localized in one or two major areas.

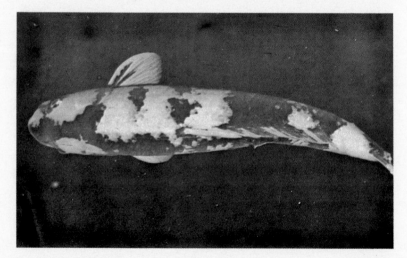

Hi-utsuri koi, but not a very good specimen.

Showa-Sanke variety.

It never gets so cold that the ponds freeze, but the koi could live under the ice without any difficulty.

Last winter the snows were so heavy and the winter so severe that the entire Yoshida farm complex was covered in snow. This didn't disturb the koi at all.

Transporting fish purchased at the auction; for comparatively long trips, the fish are sometimes placed in insulated containers.

Koi are transported from the auction to the place of business in large open tanks mounted on a truck through which oxygen is continuously bubbled.

Spectators and exhibitors jockey for viewing position at an open-air koi show in Japan. This was an international exhibition; notice the many different national flags strung on the lanyards. Photo by Dr. Herbert R. Axelrod.

Goshiki

Shusui koi; note the large scales that differentiate the Shusui from the Asagi, which has the same type of coloration.

Matsuba Ohgon koi.

The color pattern of the tricolor Taisho Sanke should be crisp and clear.

This is an unscaled, or Doitsu, type of the Taisho Sanke variety.

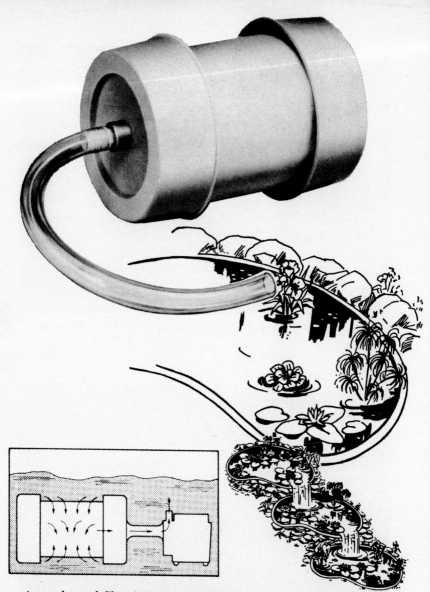

A good pond filter is important for the maintenance of a healthy pond. A pump is attached to this filter to circulate water through the unit. Filtration is accomplished by a washable, reusable foam sleeve with a filter area of approximately 200 square inches.
Courtesy of Eugene G. Danner Inc.

they were kept in a proper environment and fed well. The Japanese really consider the koi as scavengers and feed them what remains from the cocoons produced by the larvae of silk caterpillars after the silk has been removed.

Breeding koi is not usually accomplished in the goldfish pool the way goldfish breed in the pool, since the koi are too large and require too much space to become properly conditioned for breeding. In 1973 I wrote a book entitled **Koi of the World,** which is illustrated with magnificent colored photographs of nearly every recognized koi variety. This book also covers koi in much more depth than can be presented in this book. Check with your petshop or library and look through a copy of this wonderful book.

Good luck with your koi!

The pure white pectoral fins of this representative of the Kawari-Mono type contrast nicely with the bright orange color of its head.

The phosphorescent specklings of the Kohaku Gin-Lin give this koi variety an interesting iridescent appearance. Photo by the author.

Index